King Tut's Curse

William W. Lace

ReferencePoint Press®

San Diego, CA

© 2013 ReferencePoint Press, Inc.
Printed in the United States

For more information, contact:
ReferencePoint Press, Inc.
PO Box 27779
San Diego, CA 92198
www. ReferencePointPress.com

LIBRARY OF CONGRESS CATALOGING-IN-PUBLICATION DATA

Lace, William W.
  King Tut's curse / by William W. Lace.
    p. cm. -- (Ancient Egyptian wonders series)
  Includes bibliographical references and index.
  ISBN-13: 978-1-60152-250-4 (hardback)
  ISBN-10: 1-60152-250-9 (hardback)
  1. Tutankhamen, King of Egypt. 2. Tutankhamen, King of Egypt--Tomb. 3. Excavations (Archaeology)--Egypt--Valley of the Kings. 4. Valley of the Kings (Egypt)--Antiquities. 5. Carnarvon, George Edward Stanhope Molyneux Herbert, Earl of, 1866-1923--Death and burial. I. Title. II. Series: Ancient Egyptian wonders series.
  DT87.5.L34 2012
  932'.014--dc23
                                                    2011048987

CONTENTS

A Timeline of Ancient Egypt   4

Introduction   6
Death and His Lordship

Chapter One   10
The Boy King

Chapter Two   25
Search and Discovery

Chapter Three   40
The Story Takes Hold

Chapter Four   55
Natural or Supernatural?

Source Notes   69

For Further Research   73

Index   75

Picture Credits   79

About the Author   80

A TIMELINE OF ANCIENT EGYPT

Editor's note: Dates for major events and periods in ancient Egyptian history vary widely. Dates used here coincide with a timeline compiled by John Baines, professor of Egyptology at University of Oxford in England.

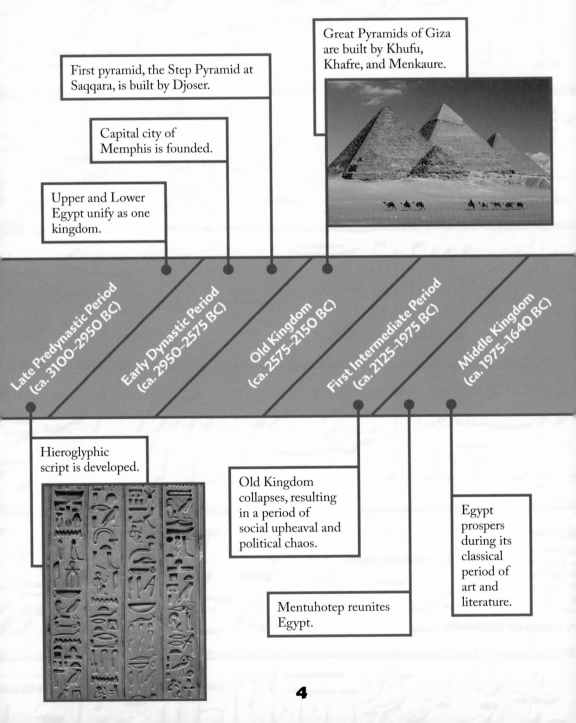

Great Pyramids of Giza are built by Khufu, Khafre, and Menkaure.

First pyramid, the Step Pyramid at Saqqara, is built by Djoser.

Capital city of Memphis is founded.

Upper and Lower Egypt unify as one kingdom.

Late Predynastic Period (ca. 3100–2950 BC)

Early Dynastic Period (ca. 2950–2575 BC)

Old Kingdom (ca. 2575–2150 BC)

First Intermediate Period (ca. 2125–1975 BC)

Middle Kingdom (ca. 1975–1640 BC)

Hieroglyphic script is developed.

Old Kingdom collapses, resulting in a period of social upheaval and political chaos.

Egypt prospers during its classical period of art and literature.

Mentuhotep reunites Egypt.

4

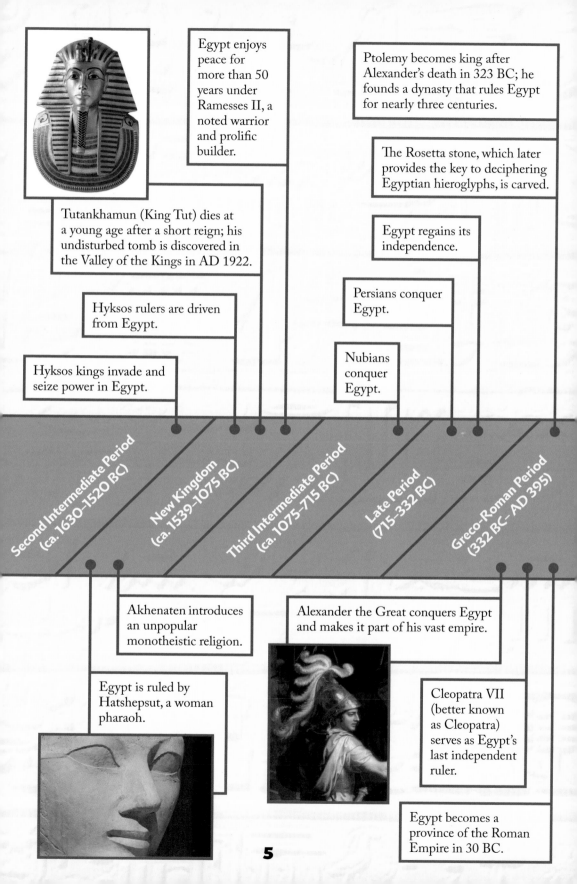

Egypt enjoys peace for more than 50 years under Ramesses II, a noted warrior and prolific builder.

Ptolemy becomes king after Alexander's death in 323 BC; he founds a dynasty that rules Egypt for nearly three centuries.

The Rosetta stone, which later provides the key to deciphering Egyptian hieroglyphs, is carved.

Tutankhamun (King Tut) dies at a young age after a short reign; his undisturbed tomb is discovered in the Valley of the Kings in AD 1922.

Egypt regains its independence.

Hyksos rulers are driven from Egypt.

Persians conquer Egypt.

Hyksos kings invade and seize power in Egypt.

Nubians conquer Egypt.

Second Intermediate Period (ca. 1630–1520 BC)

New Kingdom (ca. 1539–1075 BC)

Third Intermediate Period (ca. 1075–715 BC)

Late Period (715–332 BC)

Greco-Roman Period (332 BC– AD 395)

Akhenaten introduces an unpopular monotheistic religion.

Alexander the Great conquers Egypt and makes it part of his vast empire.

Egypt is ruled by Hatshepsut, a woman pharaoh.

Cleopatra VII (better known as Cleopatra) serves as Egypt's last independent ruler.

Egypt becomes a province of the Roman Empire in 30 BC.

INTRODUCTION

Death and His Lordship

George Edward Stanhope Molyneux Herbert, fifth Earl of Carnarvon, should have been among the happiest and most contented of men. He was rich, master of a vast estate in England, and a breeder of champion racehorses. He was famous, having joined with archaeologist Howard Carter in the discovery of the fabulous tomb of King Tutankhamun—"King Tut"—in Egypt in November 1922.

Five months after that astounding find, however, the earl was miserable. His health, frail since a serious automobile accident years earlier, had suffered from the searing desert heat, the excitement, and the strain of dealing with the hordes of visitors and newspaper reporters who flocked to the tomb.

> **DID YOU KNOW?**
> Stories about Lord Carnarvon's death in Cairo newspapers were surrounded by thick black borders as a sign of respect for the man Egyptians liked and knew as "Lordy."

Archaeologist Howard Carter and his patron Lord Carnarvon discovered the undisturbed tomb of Egypt's boy king, Tutankhamun, in 1922. Some believe that the discovery of his tomb (shown in a recent photograph) may have cost the lives of Carnarvon and others associated with the find.

On top of everything, a mosquito bite on his cheek, which he suffered sometime during the closing of the tomb for the 1922–1923 archaeological season, had become infected after he nicked it while shaving. The earl developed a high fever and swollen glands. He was treated at his hotel in Luxor, the city across the Nile River from where the tomb lay, by a doctor who advised him to stay in bed for several days. A few days later, much improved, he ignored the advice and went north to the Egyptian capital of Cairo.

"SECRET POISONS"

Now, early on the morning of April 6, 1923, Lord Carnarvon lay near death. His condition had grown steadily worse, and reports of his illness had made news worldwide. A woman named Mary Mackay, who called herself Marie Corelli and claimed to have lived before as a princess in ancient Egypt, wrote a letter to the *New York Times*. In the letter she claimed to have a rare book saying that anyone entering a sealed tomb would suffer fearful punishment. She wrote that the book describes "secret poisons enclosed in boxes in such wise [ways] that those who touch them shall not know how they come to suffer." She then added, "That is why I ask, Was it a mosquito bite that has so seriously affected Lord Carnarvon?" Furthermore, according to Corelli, the book contained a curse: "Death comes on wings to he who enters the tomb of a pharaoh."[1] What book this might have been remains a mystery. No such book has ever been found.

> **DID YOU KNOW?**
> On the day before he died, Lord Carnarvon had accepted his fate. He told a friend that he knew that his death was near and that he was ready to face it.

THE FAMILY GATHERS

Meanwhile, Carnarvon grew weaker. His wife, Lady Almina, stayed by his bedside at the Hotel Continental. His sister was nearby, as was his daughter. His private secretary, Richard Bethell, sent a telegram to Carter in Luxor telling him that Carnarvon was "gravely ill."[2]

Carter hurried to Cairo and was soon joined on April 5 by Carnarvon's son, Henry, who had rushed to Egypt from India when he received a telegram from Bethell. Henry visited his unconscious father's room and later, exhausted from his journey, went to bed. He was awakened at about 2 a.m. by a nurse who told him his father had died.

At the moment of Carnarvon's death, his son later wrote, "all the lights (in the hotel) suddenly went out."[3] Later he reported that, back at Highclere, the late earl's palatial castle, Carnarvon's favorite dog began to howl and toppled over dead.

The news of Carnarvon's death and the stories of the hotel lights and the dog spread quickly, as if on Marie Corelli's wings of death. The legend of the curse of King Tut had been born.

CHAPTER 1

The Boy King

Images of Tutankhamun that have survived the almost 3,500 years since his death sometimes portray him as a mighty warrior, wielding bow and arrow from a war chariot, or as a hunter casting a spear at his prey. He likely was never anything of the sort; rather, he was a frail teenager, a king in name only who was ruled by others.

Of the more than 300 pharaohs who ruled Egypt until it became a Roman province in 30 BC, Tutankhamun was among the least significant. Until fairly recent times, scholars were unsure whether he had even existed. Even now they dispute such basic facts as when he was born and whose son he was. Yet because of the richness of his tomb and the story of the curse that surrounds it, he ranks as the most famous of them all.

Although Tutankhamun appears to have been sickly, he came from a long line of warrior kings in the Eighteenth Dynasty, or ruling family. Ahmose, founder of the dynasty, became pharaoh by driving out foreign invaders known as the Hyksos around 1539 BC.

Under Ahmose's successors, notably Amenhotep I, II, and III and Thutmose I and III, Egypt carved out an empire stretching from present-day Sudan northward through the Sinai Peninsula, Israel, and Syria to the Euphrates River. Even rulers of ancient kingdoms such as Mitanni and Babylon, which were not under direct Egyptian control, recognized the might of the pharaohs and sent tribute, often including their daughters to be part of the royal harem.

This line of heroes seemed destined to continue until the crown prince Thutmose, eldest son of Amenhotep III and already a seasoned soldier, died prematurely, possibly in a hunting accident. So it was that, in 1353 BC, the throne passed to a younger son, Amenhotep IV.

A Different Pharaoh

The new pharaoh was not warlike by nature and hoped that Egypt's might would allow it to impose a lasting peace throughout North Africa and the Middle East. Instead of raising armies, he raised great temples at Karnak, located near the capital city of Thebes—the present-day city of Luxor.

These temples did not, however, honor Amun (also spelled Amen), the patron god of Thebes who had been merged with the sun god Ra to form Amun-Ra, king of the gods. Instead, they glorified Aten, the sun disk. Aten had been considered an aspect of Ra and had been a favorite of Amenhotep's father and grandfather; however, Amenhotep was fanatical to the point where he eventually declared that Aten was not only the supreme god but also the only god.

Such a stance naturally placed Amenhotep in opposition to the powerful and wealthy priests of Amun. But instead of confronting them, he decided to leave them and their traditional ways behind and to build a new capital in which Aten alone would rule. He changed his name from Amenhotep to Akhenaten, meaning "Transfigured Spirit of the Aten." He packed up the entire royal court—relatives, courtiers, servants, musicians, artisans, priests, wives, and children—and moved about 300 miles north down the Nile to where he constructed the new city of Akhetaten, the "Horizon of the Aten."

Tutankhamun's Parentage

It was probably here in about 1343 BC that Tutankhamun, who at the time was named Tutankhaten, was born. Until fairly recently many experts doubted that he was Akhenaten's son, but a 2008 analysis

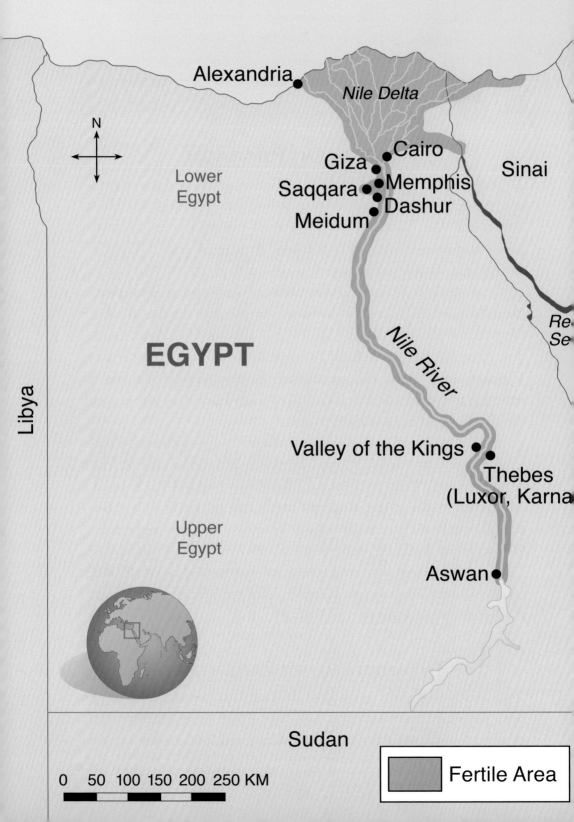

of DNA from the mummies of Tutankhamun and Akhenaten confirmed with reasonable certainty that they were father and son.

Tutankhamun's mother, however, was not Nefertiti, the pharaoh's beautiful and powerful Great Royal Wife (there was no ancient Egyptian word for *queen*). Nefertiti bore Akhenaten six daughters, whose likenesses survive in carvings, but no sons.

Tutankhamun's mother was long believed, rather, to have been Kiya, a princess from Mitanni and one of Akhenaten's lesser wives. However, the DNA tests in 2008 revealed that a mummy previously known to archaeologists as the "Younger Lady," was a daughter of Amenhotep III, a sister of Akhenaten, and also was Tutankhamun's mother.

> **DID YOU KNOW?**
> The first pharaoh to be buried in the Valley of the Kings was Thutmose I in 1492 BC. The last was probably Ramesses X about 400 years later.

For Tutankhamun's parents to have been brother and sister was not at all unusual for Egyptian royalty, who frequently married within the family in order to maintain the purity of what they considered to be a sacred bloodline.

RELIGIOUS CONFLICT

No details of Tutankhamun's early childhood have survived. He would have lived a peaceful, sheltered life in Akhetaten, knowing little about the struggle for power between his father and the priests of Amun. Sometime around the time of Tutankhamun's birth, Akhenaten began direct action against the old religion, ordering that the names of Amun and other gods be obliterated from monuments throughout Egypt. He even ordered that the name of his father, Amenhotep, be erased because it contained the name of the rival god.

Most Egyptians had clung to the old religion, and Akhenaten's actions amounted to blasphemy in their eyes. When the temples of the old gods were ordered closed, the priests simply went into hiding and the people worshipped as they always had, but in secret.

THE FIVE NAMES OF THE PHARAOH

In Tutankhamun's time, during the coronation ritual a new pharaoh adopted a titulary, consisting of five names, which had been carefully selected by scribes. The first name represented Horus, the heavenly falcon. The second stood for Wadjet and Nekhbet, the patron goddesses of Egypt when it was united in about 3100 BC. The third linked the new ruler with eternity, the fourth described him as king of Upper and Lower Egypt, and the fifth—the nomen—was the name the pharaoh already bore.

The names bestowed on Tutankhamun were Ka-na-kht tut-mesut (Strong Bull of Perfect Birth), Nefer Hepu Segereh Taui (He of the Good Laws, Who Pacifies the Two Lands), Wetches Khau Sehotep Neteru (He Who Wears the Crowns and Satisfies the Gods), Nebkheperura (All the Transformations of Ra), and finally Tutankhamun (Living Image of Amun).

Akhenaten gradually withdrew from public life. He was content to stay in his new city, worship his god, and leave governing to others. The affairs of Egypt and its relations with other kingdoms were increasingly directed by the priest Ay, thought to have been Nefertiti's father, and Horemheb, an army general.

SMENKHKARE

In about 1334 BC Akhenaten proclaimed a co-ruler named Smenkhkare. Who he was remains a mystery. Some historians believe Smenkhkare was not a man at all but a woman—Nefertiti—with whom her husband decided to share the throne. Most experts, however, now think that he might have been an older brother of Tutankhamun.

Smenkhkare's rule was a short one. No one knows exactly how short, for there is no record of him having succeeded Akhenaten when the latter died in about 1332 BC. He likely had already died, because the throne immediately passed to a boy about 10 or 11 years of age—Tutankhamun.

Akhenaten's vision of a universal religion under Aten died with him, but it was a slow death. Ay and Horemheb had been faithful to their pharaoh but not to his god. These realistic and ambitious men began a gradual process of returning Egypt to its traditional ways, and young Tutankhamun was part of their plan.

THE RESTORATION STELE

Egypt, they decided, had to be shown that it had a new pharaoh and that this pharaoh fully acknowledged and would restore Amun and all the other old gods. Within a few months of Akhenaten's death, the Restoration Stele, a large stone tablet bearing carvings, had been prominently installed at Karnak. Its message was inescapable. Without referring to Akhenaten by name, the inscription made it clear that Egypt had been through a time of great trouble but that harmony would be restored by the new pharaoh.

At the top, Tutankhamun was pictured worshipping the god Amun. Below, the inscription called Tutankhamun "the effective King who did what was good for his father [Amun] and all the gods. He restored everything that was ruined, to be his monument forever. He has vanquished chaos and has restored Ma'at [goddess of harmony] to her place." The inscription went on to describe how the traditional gods had deserted Egypt during Akhenaten's rule: "Their shrines had tumbled down, turned into piles of rubble and overgrown with weeds. . . . The world was chaotic and the gods had turned their backs on this land." However, thanks to Tutankhamun, "now the gods and goddesses of this land are rejoicing in their hearts, the Lords of the temples are in joy, the provinces all rejoice and celebrate throughout this whole land because good has come back into existence."[4]

THE KING IS CROWNED

Shortly thereafter, Egypt got its first look at the new ruler when he was formally crowned. Young Tutankhamun, who would still go by the name Tutankhaten for a time, was brought up the Nile from his father's city to either Thebes or Memphis to take part in the ancient ritual. He was probably accompanied by his future bride and half sister, Ankhesenpaaten, one of the six daughters of Akhenaten and Nefertiti.

DID YOU KNOW?
Egyptians buried their dead in the "red land," or desert. The "black land" on either side of the Nile River was considered both too damp and too essential for farming.

Because a pharaoh was considered to be a god in mortal form, the coronation ceremony involved a welcome from other gods. When the new pharaoh's barge reached the shore, he would have been welcomed by priests dressed and masked as the gods they represented. He would be led into a temple where water would be poured on him four times. Then, having been purified, he would be crowned, dressed in a white robe, and taken before the god Amun, who would proclaim him his son.

How many crowns were used in Tutankhamun's ceremony is not known, but it was very likely more than one. Pharaohs normally wore multiple crowns, although not all at once, to designate specific portions of their rule. There was the cone-shaped White Crown for Upper Egypt, the southern part of the Nile. It would fit inside the Red Crown of Lower, or northern, Egypt. The two crowns together were called the Sekhemti, or "Two Powerful Ones."

Other crowns may have played separate parts in the ceremony. The Kepresh was the Blue Crown, sometimes called the War Crown. It was of blue leather dotted with a golden sun disk and

A painted limestone tomb decoration depicts Tutankhamun (right) standing before Osiris, god of the dead. In this image, the king wears the Blue Crown—one of many crowns worn by Egypt's pharaohs.

surmounted on the front by a cobra. More likely to have been present was the Atef crown, which was a variation of the White Crown decorated on each side with ostrich feathers representing Osiris, god of the dead.

GOING BEFORE THE PEOPLE

Once the ceremony was over it would have been the people's turn to see their god-king. Tutankhamun would board the royal barge once more, this time wearing a crown, and be carried in triumph along the river. He would be accompanied by priests, a clear sign to the people that all was well with the gods.

All was not yet well with Egypt, however. The young king and his bride-to-be were returned to Akhetaten, his father's city, to remain out of sight while Ay and Horemheb worked feverishly to restore confidence and stability and to make the promises on the Restoration Stele come true.

The temples of the old gods, fallen into disrepair during Akhenaten's reign, were rebuilt, along with many other public buildings. Statues appeared by the dozens showing Tutankhamun with Amun, Mut, and the other gods whom his father had tried to abolish.

MILITARY ACTIVITY

Militarily, Horemheb's armies conducted campaigns designed to show the world that Egypt was once more a mighty power and to resume the flow of riches that had dwindled to a thin stream under Akhenaten. The campaign to the south, against the Land of Kush, or Nubia, was highly successful. The story was different in the north. The Restoration Stele admitted that, in Akhenaten's time, the country was too weak to send a major military force to rally their former allies into resisting the growing power of the Hittites who ruled what is now modern-day Turkey.

Ay and Horemheb seem to have disliked and distrusted one another, but necessity forced them to work together on Tutankhamun's behalf. Meanwhile, the young pharaoh married his half sister, and they seem to have lived peacefully in Akhetaten, surrounded by a royal court that was growing steadily smaller.

Artifacts found by archaeologists at Akhetaten indicate that the royal couple lived in a palace on the northern side of the city. During this time, the rest of the city was slowly being dismantled. Temples to Aten were torn down, not so much out of revenge but rather to reclaim the building materials for other projects. Furniture, tools and other goods were carted off to royal residences elsewhere. The people, likewise, drifted away. The time of Aten was over, the old gods had been restored, and Thebes would once more be the country's center of power.

Distinct facial features can be seen in the mummified head of King Tut. A 1960s X-ray of Tut's skull revealed what appeared to be a head wound, fueling speculation that the young king might have been murdered. A later CT scan showed otherwise.

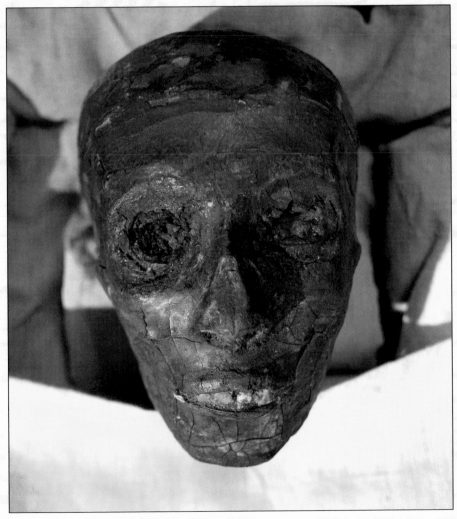

RETURN TO THEBES

In about the third year of Tutankhamun's reign, Ay and Horemheb decided it was time for the pharaoh to return to his capital, Thebes. They chose their timing carefully, making it coincide with the reconsecration of the great temples at Karnak and nearby Thebes and with a prominent religious event—Opet. This was an eleven-day festival dedicated to Amun. Opet had not been celebrated in Thebes since before the reign of Akhenaten, and the population surely welcomed its return.

Ay and the priests of Amun made sure that Tutankhamun's return and the accompanying festivities were as lavish as possible. So that the people would remember the occasion, the planners had scenes depicting it painted on two walls at Thebes.

DID YOU KNOW?

After Tutankhamun's death, his widow wrote to the king of the Hittites, asking that he send one of his sons to wed her and become pharaoh. A Hittite prince was sent but was murdered en route, probably on Horemheb's orders.

The royal barge, accompanied by several lesser craft, first went to Karnak. There, Tutankhamun wafted incense over the statues of Amun, his wife Mut, and their son Khonsu, and he decorated them with flowers. Afterward, the statues were placed in small ceremonial boats and carried to their barges.

The flotilla then headed south to Luxor, towed with ropes manned by sailors walking along the shore as soldiers held back the crowds. At one point Tutankhamun took hold of an oar, symbolizing his personal responsibility for the journey of the gods between the temples.

A TIME FOR CELEBRATION

Once at Thebes, the gods were carried into their temples, whereupon the public festival began in earnest. For 11 days the public partook of free food, wine, and beer paid for by the pharaoh and the priests of Amun. There were various forms of revelry, including dancing and public entertainments.

At the end of it all, the ceremonial voyage was repeated, and the gods returned to their Karnak temples. The pharaoh, the son of Amun, had ceremonially met his father and mother and, having done so, was ready to rule. Tutankhamun, who would formally take that name and

FROM KING TO MUMMY

The ancient Egyptians considered preservation of the earthly body necessary for a person to maintain existence in the afterlife. The preservation and burial of a pharaoh's body was doubly important because he was considered a god.

First, the embalmers used a long metal tool to extract the brain through the nostrils. Next, through an incision in the abdomen, the internal organs were removed. Only the heart, considered the source of a person's spirit, would eventually be returned to the body.

To remove all moisture from the body, it was immersed in natron, a naturally occurring salt, for 70 days. After this the inside of the body cavity was coated with resin as a preservative, and the heart—now dried and wrapped in linen—was restored. The embalmers then stuffed the cavity with resin-soaked linen to maintain its shape before closing the incision.

At this point, the body was ready to be wrapped, a process involving hundreds of yards of the finest linen into which charms and jewels were inserted. Finally, after being given a golden belt around his waist with a ceremonial dagger to fight off demons, Tutankhamun's mummy was ready for burial.

abandon the *-aten* suffix about two years later, took up residence at the royal palace in Thebes with his wife, now named Ankhesenamun.

Almost nothing is known about his personal life for the duration of his reign, which lasted about six more years. The couple had two children—both daughters and both born dead.

TUTANKHAMUN'S DEATH

In about 1325 Tutankhamun suddenly died. He was only about 18 years old. How he died has long been a matter for speculation. A head wound was revealed when his mummy was x-rayed in 1968, and it was thought he might have been murdered. The logical suspect was Ay, who eventually became pharaoh because Tutankhamun had no heir.

The question remains, however, why Ay would have felt the need to assassinate Tutankhamun. As science was to show, the pharaoh was in poor health and, after two stillbirths, seemed unlikely to have heirs. There are at least two theories. The first proposes that Ay, who was probably in his midforties—an advanced age for the time—simply was not willing to wait for his king's death. The second takes the line that Tutankhamun, having grown out of adolescence, was attempting to throw off Ay's dominance and needed to be done away with.

In 2005, however, the mummy was subjected to a CT scan, which showed that the hole in the skull had occurred long after the body was buried, probably as it was moved by archaeologists shortly after its discovery. The scan also showed that Tutankhamun had suffered a broken femur, or thigh bone, a short time before his death, perhaps from a hunting accident. Some experts speculate that he might have died from an infection resulting from the break.

DNA PROVIDES NEW INFORMATION

The more recent analysis of the mummy's DNA, however, has shed considerable light on both Tutankhamun's physical condition and the true cause of this death. For one thing, he was probably not a hunter. "He was not a very strong pharaoh. He was not riding the chariots," says Carsten

Pusch, one of the scientists on the DNA project. "Picture instead a frail, weak boy who had a bit of a club foot and who needed a cane to walk."[5]

There had been clues as to his condition. More than 100 walking sticks had been found in his tomb. Moreover, some carvings and paintings had shown him seated for activities at which most pharaohs were pictured standing.

The foot disorder was likely due to avascular necrosis, a disease in which bone tissue dies when it somehow loses its blood supply. Although this would have crippled Tutankhamun, it probably would not have killed him. The DNA analysis, however, revealed another culprit: malaria.

The scientists found, in addition to the pharaoh's DNA, other DNA from the malaria-causing parasite *Plasmodium falciparum*. Multiple strains of this DNA were found, indicating that he had suffered repeated, severe bouts of malaria.

But Zahi Hawass, Egypt's minister of state for antiquities, thinks that malaria was perhaps only a contributing factor, though an important one, to the king's death. "In my view," he wrote, "Tutankhamun's health was compromised from the moment he was conceived. . . . Married siblings are more likely to pass along twin copies of harmful genes, leaving their children vulnerable to a variety of genetic defects."[6] It was this vulnerability, Hawass concluded, that led Tutankhamun eventually to die of causes from which others might have survived.

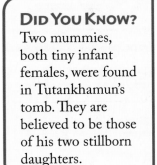

DID YOU KNOW?
Two mummies, both tiny infant females, were found in Tutankhamun's tomb. They are believed to be those of his two stillborn daughters.

QUESTIONS REMAIN

The circumstances of Tutankhamun's death thus may have been proven, but those connected with his burial remain. His tomb is unusually small, about 1,000 square feet, or less than half the usual size for pharaohs of that time. It was hardly the monument to its occupant's glory that was the intent of other royal tombs. It also shows signs of having been hastily completed. Chalk marks made by masons were left on walls, and smudges on paintings show they may not have had time to dry.

Archaeologists suspect that the tomb may not have been intended for Tutankhamun at all. Some believe that it was taken over and used out of a desire to see the young king buried as quickly and quietly as possible. A possible reason, proposed by Egyptologist Christine El Mahdy, was that Ay wanted Tutankhamun buried and himself proclaimed pharaoh before Horemheb, who probably thought himself next in line, had a chance to do anything about it.

Royal tombs were intended not only to reflect the might of pharaohs but also to provide them an eternal resting place. Such rest, however, was almost always disturbed by grave robbers, and Tutankhamun's tomb was no exception. It was broken into twice less than four years after his death. The doors were resealed each time, and after the second robbery, the stairs leading down into the tomb were buried in the hope that its location would be lost.

THE LOST TOMB

And lost it was. About 200 years later, during the building of Ramesses VI's tomb, workmen constructed their stone huts directly on top of the entrance. Not only had the tomb been forgotten, but for the most part Tutankhamun himself had been as well. Ay ruled only about four years and was succeeded by Horemheb. The former general then set out to erase all records of the three kings who had preceded him—Akhenaten, Tutankhamun, and Ay—by destroying some of their monuments or substituting his name for theirs on others.

With most of the physical reminders of his reign gone, the boy pharaoh faded from memory, existing only as an obscure and largely unknown entry in a long list of rulers. He would remain so for more than 3,000 years.

CHAPTER 2

Search and Discovery

Howard Carter and Lord Carnarvon shared many things, among them a passion for Egypt, a conviction that a royal tomb could be found, and the persistence to seek it out. Fortunately, each could also furnish what the other lacked. Carter had expertise, and Carnarvon had money. Their partnership would make possible the most important archaeological discovery of the century and also one of the most enduring mysteries.

Carter came from a far different social and economic background than did the wealthy, titled Carnarvon. He was born in the small English village of Swaffham, about 100 miles northeast of London. His father, a painter who specialized in portraits of well-to-do families' pets, could not afford to send him to school. Instead, Carter was tutored at home, learning not only reading, writing, and math but also how to draw and paint. As a boy he sometimes earned pocket money by doing watercolors of family pets in the area.

In 1890 archaeologist Percy Newberry, who was visiting the estate of one of Carter's father's clients, happened to mention that he was in need of someone to help finish drawings from Egyptian tombs that had been done the previous year. The client, Lady Amherst, recommended the 17-year-old Carter. Newberry lost no time in arranging an interview, and within a few weeks Carter was working at London's British Museum.

OFF TO EGYPT

He would not stay long in London. Only three months later, impressed by his work, the museum sent him to Egypt. There, he became an assistant to Flinders Petrie, possibly the world's foremost Egyptologist of that time.

Ancient Egypt had long fascinated visitors and scholars from throughout the world, but it had been only recently—in archaeological terms—that much was known about the civilization that had built the Great Pyramids and pioneered the art of writing on paper. The problem was that no one could decipher what was on that paper or on the hundreds of carvings. That changed in 1799 when a French soldier discovered the Rosetta stone. This tablet, with the same text carved in Egyptian hieroglyphics, or picture writing, and two other languages, including Greek, at last provided the key to translation.

Carter spent six years working with Petrie copying paintings and carvings while absorbing the science of archaeology from Petrie and his colleagues. Above all, he learned how meticulous, patient, and painstaking one had to be. "Most people think of excavating as a pleasant holiday amusement," Petrie once remarked. "Just walking about a place and finding things."[7]

His education was not all about strenuous, tedious, and frequently unproductive work. The blunt, often withdrawn Carter also had a romantic streak. He sometimes indulged it by climbing to the top of a tower at the temple of the pharaoh Ramesses III after dark and looking west at the moonlit Valley of the Kings, where so many rulers had been buried. On another occasion, he was moved to kneel at the temple of Amun-Ra at Karnak and dip his hands in the sacred pool whose waters once were used to ceremonially wash the bodies of dead pharaohs. Carter was falling in love with Egypt.

Within the dry, brown hills of the seemingly unremarkable Valley of the Kings (pictured) lie the tombs of many of Egypt's great pharaohs. Howard Carter was fascinated by this landscape and the treasures it held.

His dedication and enthusiasm impressed his superiors, including Sir Gaston Maspero, director of the Egyptian Antiquities Service. In 1899, although only 25, Carter was appointed by Maspero to be inspector in chief of Upper Egypt, from Thebes southward. He was thus in charge of some of the most productive archaeological sites in the country, including the Valley of the Kings.

In 1902, while still an inspector, Carter also began working with Theodore Davis, a wealthy American amateur archaeologist who had been searching the Valley of the Kings with great enthusiasm but without much in the way of planning. Davis's dream, one shared by all Egyptologists, was to find an intact, unplundered pharaonic tomb. Most experts, however, thought such a dream would never become reality. First, most pharaohs already had been accounted for, many of them discovered in 1875 in a cache of about 40 mummies that probably had

COUNTERING CRITICISM

Angered when Lord Carnarvon gave exclusive coverage of Tutankhamun's tomb to the *Times* of London, reporters from other newspapers began to criticize him and Carter for invading the sanctity of the burial chamber, hinting that nothing but evil could come of it. In reply, the *Times* ran an article quoting an "eminent Egyptologist," probably Jean Capart, who defended the efforts of Carter and Carnarvon:

> Some people are seized with pity for the hapless fate of poor King Tutankhamun, who finds himself disturbed in his earthly rest by the curiosity of archaeologists. To hear them, one ought immediately to restore the protective walls behind which he has escaped the seekers for treasure . . . [but] something more than the groans of neurasthenics [people suffering from a psychological disorder] and lunatics is necessary to convince me that the Egyptologists are violating the secret of death in a sacrilegious manner.

Quoted in Thomas Hoving, *Tutankhamun: The Untold Story*. New York: Simon & Schuster, 1978, p. 209.

been taken from their tombs and buried secretly by priests in an effort to save them from desecration by robbers. Second, even if a new tomb were discovered, it most likely would have been emptied centuries ago as so many others had been.

THE MISSING PHARAOH

Davis and Carter were unconvinced. Carter especially was hopeful that the tomb of one of the pharaohs unaccounted for—Tutankhamun—would still be found. In 1903, working in Carter's systematic style, the pair made a significant discovery: the tomb of Thutmose IV, Akhenaten's grandfather. But the discovery was not as significant as Carter and Davis had hoped. Although the tomb contained many important artifacts, it had been stripped by robbers of the most valuable pieces. In addition, Thutmosis's mummy was nowhere to be found.

Davis continued searching and in 1908 discovered the largely empty tomb of Horemheb, after which he said, "I fear that the Valley of the Kings is now exhausted."[8]

This discovery, however, was not made with Carter's help. Late in 1903, when Petrie and a group of female students were excavating a site at Saqqara, a group of drunken French tourists came into their camp at night demanding a tour. When they tried to force their way into the women's huts, Petrie summoned Carter, who arrived with an escort of Egyptian guards. A fight broke out, and one of the guards knocked a Frenchman to the ground. The Frenchmen left, but he later filed a formal complaint against Carter. The French ambassador demanded an apology, which the stubborn Carter refused to give despite Maspero's repeated urging. Finally, to bring an end to what had become an international incident, Maspero reluctantly dismissed Carter from the Antiquities Service.

Having no desire to return to England, Carter stayed in Egypt, sometimes living with men who had been his foremen on digs and doing occasional odd jobs for Petrie and Davis. To supplement a meager and sporadic income, he painted and sold watercolors to tourists.

LORD CARNARVON

Carter's dismissal coincided with the arrival in Egypt of Lord Carnarvon, who had more or less drifted through life as an aristocratic playboy. That idle existence changed radically when he suffered life-threatening injuries in an automobile accident. Doctors advised him to forgo the damp, cold English winters for the dry climate of Egypt.

He started out as a collector of ancient artifacts and then, like many others before him, wanted to try digging for them himself. He obtained an excavation permit in 1906 and soon became an enthusiastic, if undisciplined, amateur archaeologist. His first attempt produced only a mummified cat, a poor reward for what he called "strenuous and very dusty endeavours."[9]

Carnarvon decided that he needed professional help, and Maspero knew just the man: Howard Carter. Enough time had elapsed since the Saqqara incident, Maspero thought, for French tempers to have cooled. He arranged for a meeting, and the partnership was formed.

THE WORK BEGINS

Carter and Carnarvon began work in 1907, but not in the Valley of the Kings. Davis still had exclusive rights there and soon found what he thought was the tomb of Tutankhamun. He had found a blue cup bearing Tutankhamun's name the year before and, on returning to the site, discovered a tomb about 25 feet below the surface. There was no mummy or coffin, but there were several pieces of gold foil bearing the names of Tutankhamun and his wife and also an alabaster statue of a young man. In addition, some earthen jars were discovered nearby, one of them wrapped with a cloth carrying Tutankhamun's name.

Davis claimed to have found Tutankhamun's tomb, but Carter knew better. The tomb, he thought, was far too small for any pharaoh, however minor. Nonetheless, Davis's discoveries convinced Carter that the boy king had been buried in the Valley of the Kings and that his tomb remained to be found.

> **DID YOU KNOW?**
> Correspondents covering the removal of items from the tomb would, at day's end, ride donkeys, horses, or camels in a race to be first to telegraph their articles from Luxor.

Davis finally abandoned his digging in 1912, and his rights to the Valley of the Kings were taken up by Carnarvon. The contract was drawn up in 1914, but World War I was under way; excavation would have to wait until 1917, when the threat of military action in Egypt had ceased. Carter began by dividing the Valley of the Kings into grids.

WHERE TO BEGIN?

"The difficulty," Carter wrote, "was to know where to begin, for mountains of rubbish thrown out by previous excavators encumbered the ground in all directions."[10] Carter's strategy, as a result, was to dig all the way down to bedrock in the area—a triangle of about two and one-half acres—where he thought Tutankhamun's tomb was most likely to be found.

Carter dug alone that first season, concentrating on a section near the tomb of Ramesses VI. This was the area where Davis had found links to Tutankhamun and where Carter thought the tomb might lie. About 15 yards from the tomb's entrance, he uncovered the ancient foundations of the huts occupied by the builders of Ramesses's tomb. The huts had been built on a layer of limestone boulders. Such boulders might have been a clue to the building of another tomb in the area. Carter, however, did not investigate and moved to another grid. The season ended with nothing of value found.

Carnarvon joined the effort the next year. The entire triangle was cleared of debris down to bedrock, but they found nothing except some alabaster jars bearing the names of the pharaohs Ramesses II and Merenptah. The next three seasons—1919 through 1921—produced nothing, but an exciting and encouraging discovery was to come from an unlikely source: the United States.

WINLOCK'S DISCOVERY

Herbert Winlock of the Metropolitan Museum of Art in New York City had gotten around to studying the artifacts found by Davis back in 1907. He noticed what others had overlooked. Some of the items carried not only Tutankhamun's name but also the seal of the royal necropolis, or city of the dead. This, to Winlock, was clear proof that the young pharaoh had been buried in the Valley of the Kings.

Moreover, when he examined the contents of the jars found nearby, he was able to deduce that they contained remnants, including food scraps, dishes, and bits of floral wreaths and linen headbands, of a ceremonial funeral banquet that would have been held in a tomb. Carter now was sure that Tutankhamun's tomb was in the immediate vicinity, quite possibly under the foundations of the workers' huts.

However, when he visited Carnarvon's estate of Highclere in the summer of 1922, he received a shock. Despite Winlock's discoveries and Carter's assurances of success, Carnarvon was tired and discouraged. He told Carter that the search was growing too expensive and was at an end.

ONE LAST ATTEMPT

Carter was stunned but recovered quickly. Carnarvon's excavating permit would run out after the next season, he said, and he was willing to finance this one last attempt himself if Carnarvon would agree. The English lord was impressed with the offer but knew that the expense, the equivalent of about $50,000 today, was beyond Carter's means. He did what he considered the gentlemanly thing: he would finance one last year. Carter gratefully accepted and agreed that if nothing was found, he would concede that the Valley of the Kings had, indeed, been emptied of treasures.

Before he left England for Egypt the following fall, Carter announced to Carnarvon and to some of his associates at the British Museum that this time he would take a companion. Carter's friends wondered who this companion could be. Carter had lived alone throughout his many years in Egypt. Had he found a wife?

When he arrived in Alexandria in October, his companion was on his arm—a golden canary whose cheerful songs would delight Carter's workers. They named her "Golden Bird" and considered her a symbol of good luck.

The good luck was not long in coming. Carter arrived in Luxor on October 28, 1922, and lost no time getting to work, concentrating on the area on which the workers' huts sat near the tomb of Ramesses VI. Three days were spent removing the ancient foundations and the boulders on which they had been built. On the evening of November 3, Carter determined that there were still three feet of debris to be removed before they hit bedrock. He returned to his house, leaving instructions for work to begin early the next day.

THE DAY OF DISCOVERY

When he arrived at the worksite on the morning of November 4, he immediately noticed that all was quiet. There was none of the singing, shouting, and general turmoil that usually punctuated the workday. The silence, he wrote, "made me realize that something out of the ordinary had happened, and I was greeted by an announcement that a step cut in the rock had been discovered under the very first hut to be attacked."[11]

Years later, while on a lecture tour in the United States, Carter told a different story. His booking agent recalled him saying that everyone on the dig had almost lost hope,

> except the water boy whose stake [potential reward] was small but whose energy the sun could not penetrate or slacken. Like small, industrious boys emulating their elders he was carrying on, in his play, digging with sticks in the sand, when suddenly he hit a hard surface. He dug furiously and in a few moments had unearthed a stone step. . . . [He] then ran as fast as his legs would carry him to tell Howard Carter of what he had found.[12]

As Carter and his new assistant, A.R. "Pecky" Callender, looked on, workmen cleared the step and found that it led to another and to

TUTMANIA!

The discovery of the tomb of Tutankhamun created a sensation around the world, but particularly in Egypt. Arthur Merton of the London *Times* covered the story in 1923:

Tutankhamun, though dead, liveth and reigneth in Thebes and Luxor today. All the district is his court. His name is all over the town. It is shouted in the streets, whispered in the hotels. While in the local shops Tutankhamun advertises everything: art, hats, curios, photographs and tomorrow probably "genuine" antiquities. Every hotel in Luxor had something on the menu à la Tut. The Queen of the Belgians, though a prominent figure . . . is merely the modern queen of a nation. But to be the thing in Thebes one has got to show some, any, connection with the ancient King. Slight acquaintances buttonhole one another and tell of dreams they had yesterday of Tutankhamun. There is a Tutankhamun dance tonight at which the first piece is to be a Tutankhamun rag.

Quoted in Thomas Hoving, *Tutankhamun: The Untold Story*. New York: Simon and Schuster, 1978, p. 264.

another and so on until, by the middle of the next day, 16 steps had been revealed. At the end of the staircase stood a sealed brick door bearing the sign of the royal necropolis but giving no sign of who the occupant might have been.

Exercising Control

Carter knew that the chances were extremely slim that the tomb would be intact and unplundered, with the mummy still in place. Yet he dared to hope. "Anything, literally anything, might lie beyond that passage," he wrote, "and it needed all my self control to keep from breaking down the doorway, and investigating then and there."[13]

Instead, he made only a small hole at the top of the doorway. Looking through with the aid of a flashlight, he could see that the space on the other side was filled with rocks and rubble. It was the sign of a passageway leading to a second door, a passageway that had been filled in to deter robbers.

Carter knew that, however much he wanted to proceed, he owed it to Carnarvon that he be part of the discovery. He ordered his crew to fill in the staircase once again. Leaving Callender on watch with a loaded rifle, he went back to Luxor and arranged for Sudanese soldiers to stand guard at the tomb. He then telegraphed Carnarvon:

> **DID YOU KNOW?**
> The death penalty was unusual in Egypt but was used in ancient times for tomb robbers. The usual method was a severe beating followed by impalement on a stake.

"At last have made a wonderful discovery in valley. Magnificent tomb with seals intact. Recovered same for your arrival. Congratulations."[14]

Carnarvon, on receiving the telegram, immediately made plans to travel to Egypt, cabling Carter that he expected to arrive in Alexandria in two weeks. On November 18 Carter left Luxor for Cairo, where he would meet his patron. While he was gone, something happened that later led some people to think that King Tut's curse had claimed its first victim.

The Death of Golden Bird

One afternoon Callender, who was living in Carter's house, heard a high squeak and a rapid fluttering. He went into the next room and saw Golden Bird being swallowed by a cobra that had somehow managed to get into its cage. Winlock later wrote that, because cobras had long been a symbol of Egyptian royalty, "the conclusion was obvious. The King's serpent had struck at the mascot who had given away [by bringing good luck to Carter] the secret of the tomb. And the sequel was obvious . . . that before the winter was out someone would die."[15]

Another version of the event was later told by James Breasted, an Egyptologist who had just joined Carter's staff. According to Breasted's son Charles, his father said that Carter had sent a worker to collect something from his house:

> As the man approached the house he heard a faint, almost human cry. Then all was silent again—even the bird had stopped singing. Upon entering, he looked almost instinctively at the cage and saw coiled within it a cobra holding in its mouth the dead canary. News of this spread quickly and all the natives now said: "Alas, that was the King's cobra, revenging itself upon the bird for having betrayed the place of the tomb—and now something terrible will happen.[16]

CARNARVON ARRIVES

The incident was forgotten in all the excitement that greeted the arrival of Carnarvon and his daughter Evelyn. On the morning of November 26, 1922, they watched as workmen once more uncovered the stairway and, this time, also uncovered the entire door. Carter could now see several seals with the name of Tutankhamun.

With the excitement came disappointment. The door showed clear evidence that it had been entered twice shortly after the burial and resealed by priests. The tomb, therefore, was not completely intact, but at least, Carter reasoned, the robbers might have been caught and their loot restored.

After the door had been carefully removed, brick by brick, workers removed 30 feet of debris from the passageway. A second door was then revealed, as had been expected. It, too, bore the seals of Tutankhamun.

With trembling hands, Carter made a small hole in the upper left-hand corner of the door and inserted an iron rod. There was no resistance. What lay immediately behind the door was empty space. He widened the hole and held a lighted candle to the opening. There was a rush of hot air, but the candle stayed alight, indicating that there were no poisonous gases within. Carter widened the hole to the point where he could insert the candle and most of his head. It took a moment for his eyes to become adjusted to the flickering light. Then "details of the room within emerged slowly from the mist, strange animals, statues, and gold—everywhere the glint of gold."[17]

Howard Carter and Lord Carnarvon work with their assistants inside the tomb of Tutankhamun. The find was so extensive that Carter assembled a team of experts to help with the project.

For a long moment, Carter said nothing. Finally Carnarvon asked if he could see anything. "It was all I could do," Carter wrote later, "to get out the words, 'Yes, wonderful things.'"[18] He then made the hole wider so that first Evelyn, then her father, and finally Callender could see. What they saw were couches, statues, alabaster jars, golden chariots, and a golden throne. There was no sarcophagus and no mummy, but on the far side of the room was yet another door.

Carter's official version of the discovery says that the group had seen enough for one day. He wrote that he reclosed the hole, locked the first doorway with a wooden grill that had been installed, and went back to Luxor. "I think we slept but little, all of us,"[19] he recalled.

It was no wonder. The day's activities had been held under the watchful eye of a representative of the Egyptian Antiquities Service.

> **Did You Know?**
> The most prominent person to visit the tomb during the first year after it was opened was Queen Elizabeth of Belgium, who visited four times while in Egypt.

Now, late at night and free from observation, Carter, Callender, Carnarvon, and Lady Evelyn returned to the tomb. Carter removed part of the second door and wriggled through, followed by Carnarvon and his daughter. They wandered awestruck among the treasures in what would come to be known as the antechamber. Carter discovered another door that, when opened, revealed another room packed with artifacts.

Finding a King

But where was Tutankhamun? Carter finally found yet another brick door. He made another hole large enough for him and the others to edge through, though Callender, a large man, could not fit and stayed behind. The trio found themselves in the burial chamber looking at an immense shrine of blue and gold. After some hesitation, Carter opened the shrine's door to discover a second inner shrine. On its door, intact and unviolated, were the seals of the royal necropolis. Tutankha-mun had been found!

The official opening of the tomb occurred on the next morning. The archaeologists spent the next few days making observations and taking photographs, but it was clear to Carter that he would need much more help in dealing with his discovery. The doors were resealed, and a steel grate was placed over the first doorway. The first phase was complete. Carter began assembling a team of experts from throughout the world to assist with the project.

Carnarvon and his daughter returned to England. They came back to Egypt in late January 1923 to find the tomb site swarming not only with Carter and his team but also with hordes of journalists and tour-ists. Carnarvon stood the pressure as best he could, but it proved to be too much. He became irritable. He and Carter had fierce arguments. He suffered terribly from the heat. Then, in March, came the fateful mosquito bite and, in April, his death.

Carter was deeply shaken and at one point said, "This tomb has brought us bad luck."[20] That bad luck, which some would call a pha-raoh's curse from beyond the grave, would strike many others in years to come.

CHAPTER 3

The Story
Takes Hold

Mummies, curses, and mysterious deaths were nothing new to Egypt, but the worldwide interest in Tutankhamun's tomb, coupled with the death of Lord Carnarvon, created a wildfire of rumor, speculation, and exaggeration that would carry far beyond the grave. It eventually reached the point where the death of anyone connected with the pharaoh or his tomb, however remotely, only added fuel to the flames.

Curses and strange deaths had long been part of the mysterious aura surrounding ancient Egypt, and mummies in particular had become associated with evil. Accounts of a mummy's curse date back to an 1827 children's book entitled *The Mummy!* In that book, which is similar to Mary Shelley's *Frankenstein,* a mummy is brought back to life. When the revived mummy's eyes opened, they

were now fixed on those of Edric, shining with supernatural luster. In vain Edric attempted to rouse himself;—in vain to turn away from that withering glance. The mummy's eyes still pursued him with their ghastly brightness; they seemed to possess the fabled fascination of those of the rattle-snake, and though he shrank from their gaze, they still glared horribly upon him.[21]

The same theme was taken up by such well-known authors as Louisa May Alcott (*Lost in a Pyramid*) and Bram Stoker (*The Jewel of Seven Stars*). In Stoker's 1903 book, an archaeologist ignores a curse carved on a tomb door and steals a priceless ring from the mummy's hand. Sure enough, everyone associated with the jewel starts to die.

UNUSUAL DEATHS

There certainly had been no shortage of unusual deaths among Egyptologists leading up to Carnarvon's. One of the first was that of the Italian explorer Giovanni Belzoni, who discovered the tomb of Pharaoh Seti I in 1817. Writing of his adventures, Belzoni recalled, "I could not pass without putting my face in contact with that of some decayed Egyptian. . . . I could not avoid being covered with bones, legs, arms, and heads rolling from above."[22] He died of a fever in 1823 at the age of 45.

> **DID YOU KNOW?**
> Howard Carter once received a letter in which he was told that if he closed and sealed Tutankhamun's tomb and then poured oil, wine, and milk over it, the curse would be gone.

There was also Jean-François Champollion, the French scholar who deciphered the Rosetta stone in 1822. Four years later, during an expedition to Egypt, he removed a large wall panel from the tomb of Seti I. In 1832, when only 41 years old, he died of a sudden stroke.

The deaths of Ernest Harold Jones and Edward Ayrton, both of whom worked for Theodore Davis as archaeologists, occurred closer to Carnarvon's time. Ayrton served Davis from 1905 to 1908 and was key to several discoveries, including the tomb of Horemheb. He drowned during a hunting trip in 1914. Jones, who took Ayrton's place on Davis's team, died of a fever after three years spent in the Valley of the Kings.

THE CASE OF CARNARVON

Plenty of strange stories were connected with Carnarvon's death. His son later wrote that at the moment of his father's death the hospital

The Rosetta stone provided the key to understanding the hieroglyphs of ancient Egypt. The French scholar who deciphered the writings on the stone, Jean-François Champollion, died suddenly at the age of 41.

suddenly went dark. The blackout affected the entire city, and the local newspapers were quick to connect it to a curse by the spirit of Tutankhamun. Carter remarked on this to Carnarvon's son:

> The newspapers have concocted a story that the lights were put out by the express command of King Tut. They say, in effect,

that your father, an infidel, had ignored all the warnings and disturbed the sacred remains of King Tutankhamun. To uphold his sovereignty, the King has taken his vengeance and, in order that all should note his displeasure, he turned out every single light in the city of Cairo the moment your father passed away.[23]

Later, however, it seemed to some as if Tutankhamun's reach had extended not only to the Cairo electric power system but also more than 2,000 miles away to the English countryside. When the new Lord Carnarvon returned home after his father's death, he learned from a housekeeper that his father's favorite dog had died at approximately the same time as his master. "According to her . . . [the dog] sat up in her basket, howled like a wolf and fell back dead. . . . Mrs. McLean [the housekeeper] felt this curious story seemed to confirm what she had read about the alleged curse that had been put on my poor father."[24]

THE BIRD CURSES

Still another story making the rounds in Cairo was that Carnarvon, as he lay ridden with fever, complained that a bird was scratching his face. This tale, true or not, was connected with two known curses. The first, dating from about 2100 BC, said that anyone violating a tomb would have his or her face scratched by a vulture. The second, slightly older curse was carved on the tomb of Harkhuf, a governor of Upper Egypt. It read, in part, "As for any man who shall enter into this tomb . . . I will pounce upon him as on a bird; he shall be judged for it by the great god."[25]

Carnarvon's death and the stories that swirled around it were perhaps not that much of a shock to his family. After all, there had been mysterious warnings. Years earlier, as was fashionable at the time, Carnarvon had become interested in the occult. His son remembered at least two séances—small gatherings at which a medium would try to make contact with the spirit world—held at Highclere.

Shortly after Carnarvon returned to England following the initial discovery of Tutankhamun's tomb, he received a strange message. It had been sent by a well-known spiritualist named William Warner, who called himself Count Louis le Warner Hamon or "Chiero." He claimed

LIGHTS OUT!

ord Carnarvon's son tried to discover the reason for the sudden power failure in Cairo at the time of his father's death. He found none. "We asked the Cairo electric company," he recalled, "and they knew of no logical explanation for the lights going out and then on again."

More than 50 years after Carnarvon's death, his son, who had inherited his father's title on the latter's death, visited New York City. While attending a dinner party in an apartment high above Manhattan, he happened to be looking out over the brilliantly lit city when the famous New York Blackout occurred. "It is again the Curse of Tutankhamun," he said.

Quoted in Philipp Vandenberg, *The Curse of the Pharaohs*. Philadelphia: J.B. Lippincott, 1975, p. 27.

Quoted in Thomas Hoving, *Tutankhamun: The Untold Story*. New York: Simon & Schuster, 1978, p. 230.

to own a mummified hand of one of Akhenaten's daughters and that the hand had written the warning that Carnarvon was to forbid the removal of any objects from the tomb. If he did not, said the warning, "he would suffer an injury while in the tomb—a sickness from which he would never recover, and that death would claim him in Egypt."[26]

VELMA'S PREDICTION

Carnarvon vowed to go ahead with the project but was worried to the extent that he consulted his own medium, a man known only as

"Velma," asking that his palm be read. During the reading, Velma told Carnarvon that although his life line was long, it was thin in the middle and there were ominous spots nearby.

Carnarvon initially dismissed the warning, but he had another session with Velma just before leaving for Egypt. The mysterious spots, the medium said, were more intense and seemed to be at a point near the earl's present age. "If I were you," Velma said, "I should make some public excuse and finish. I can see only disaster ahead."[27]

Newspapers capitalized on the predictions of doom, reporting that there had been yet another warning, this one found in Tutankhamun's tomb itself. Carter had, indeed, found a brick on which was inscribed, "It is I who hinder the sand from choking the secret chamber."[28] In the newspaper story, however, the brick was transformed into a statue of the god Anubis, and the inscription included a curse: "and I will kill all those who cross this threshold into the sacred precincts of the Royal King who lives forever."[29]

FROM BOOK TO TABLET

This was not the only journalistic exaggeration. Marie Corelli's "wings of death" letter was revisited, and some enterprising reporters changed her story so that the warning was transformed from an ancient book to a tablet found inside the tomb.

In his book *The Curse of the Pharaohs*, Philipp Vandenberg maintains that the tablet bearing the curse was, indeed, found in Tutankhamun's tomb, but Carter and an associate named Alan Gardiner suppressed the discovery. According to Vandenberg, "They worried that the Egyptian laborers would [believe the curse], and since they were dependent on the help of native helpers, mention of the clay tablet was wiped from the written record of the tomb's discovery."[30]

> **DID YOU KNOW?**
> Professor Jean Capart of the Royal Museum of Belgium once challenged anyone claiming that a curse was written on Tutankhamun's tomb to prove its existence. No one accepted his challenge.

Such a subterfuge on Carter's part seems highly unlikely. He was, above all, a scientist and a very careful one. It would have been most unprofessional of him to omit such a find from his meticulous cataloging.

Even so, Carter never explicitly denied that such a tablet had been found. Richard Adamson, a sergeant in the British army assigned to help Carter, said the archaeologist had a good reason for perpetuating the rumor. According to Adamson, Carter hoped to protect the site, saying, "It will do wonders for security if this gets around."[31]

THE COLLECTORS PANIC

Rumors of the tablet quickly spread, setting off an avalanche of sensational reports that caused a panic among collectors of ancient Egyptian artifacts. People suddenly viewed in a new light that statue of Amun or that inscribed vase they had bought in markets in Cairo or Luxor. A London newspaper reported that "the death of Lord Carnarvon has been followed by a panic among collectors of Egyptian antiques. All over the country people are sending their treasures to the British Museum, anxious to get rid of them because of the superstition that Lord Carnarvon was killed by the 'ka' or double of the soul of Tutankhamun."[32]

> **DID YOU KNOW?**
> The most common form of curse in ancient Egypt and throughout the history of the Middle East has been to write the victim's name on a jar and then smash it.

Reporters used every angle they could find to keep the story alive. One of the most well-known followers of spiritualism in the 1920s in Britain was Sir Arthur Conan Doyle, creator of the Sherlock Holmes stories. Asked by a reporter from the *Times* of London about Carnarvon's death, Doyle said it could have been caused by a "pharaoh's curse."[33]

Had Carnarvon's death and Doyle's pronouncement been followed by a period of relative calm, the story of the curse might have died with Carnarvon. Yet such was not to be the case. Barely a month after the earl's death, American railroad tycoon George Jay Gould died of pneumonia in France only weeks after visiting Tutankhamun's tomb. Then, in September 1923, Aubrey Herbert, Carnarvon's half brother who had been present at the tomb opening, died of blood poisoning at age 43.

MORE DEATHS

Other deaths followed in rapid succession. Woolf Joel, heir to a South African diamond fortune, took time from his yachting trip up the Nile to visit the tomb. Shortly after going back on board, he disappeared. The next day he was found drowned, and suicide was suspected.

The next to die was Hugh Evelyn-White, a prominent British archaeologist who had visited the tomb in 1924. Shortly thereafter, Evelyn-White hanged himself. He left a suicide note that supposedly read, in part, "I have succumbed to a curse which forces me to disappear."[34]

One death often ascribed to King Tut's curse is that of Archibald Douglas Reed, one of the world's foremost radiologists. He supposedly was brought into the project to x-ray Tutankhamun's mummy before it was removed to a museum in Cairo. According to several accounts, Reed became ill after examining the mummy and died three days later. However, Reed actually died in January 1924, two years before the mummy was removed.

ANOTHER VICTIM

Reed may or may not have visited the tomb, but the next victim, Georges Benedite, was known to have done so. The highly respected curator of the Department of Egyptology at Paris's Louvre museum died shortly after an inspection of the tomb in 1926. He was almost 70 at the time, and his death was said to have been caused by heat stroke or a fall. One unsubstantiated version claimed that the fatal fall was on the stairs leading down into the tomb.

Another death in 1926 was linked to Tutankhamun's curse even though the person in question, Aaron Ember, had not visited the tomb.

Egyptologist Aaron Ember died in 1926 of injuries sustained in a fire at his home. According to accounts of the time, Ember was fatally injured while trying to save his work on the Egyptian Book of the Dead. *Pictured here is a page from the* Book of the Dead.

He was, however, a professor of Egyptology at Johns Hopkins University in Baltimore, Maryland, and knew several of the people connected with the discovery. Early on the morning of May 31, passersby saw smoke coming from Ember's home and tried, without success, to alert those inside. Ember's wife, son, and a maid died at the scene. The professor himself apparently could have escaped, but he had lingered to try to save a manuscript he was working on, supposedly about the Egyptian *Book of the Dead*. He died in a hospital the next day, and newspapers quickly linked his fate to those who had died before.

The curse was said to have struck again in 1928, but this time the victim had been intimately involved with Carter and the tomb. Days after the initial discovery, Carter cabled Herbert Winlock at the Metropolitan Museum of Art in New York to ask for assistance. Winlock organized an expedition that included Arthur C. Mace, a respected archaeologist and nephew of Carter's mentor, Flinders Petrie.

Mace would go on to spend six years working alongside Carter at the tomb, and in 1923 he and Carter coauthored a multivolume account of the project. According to some reports, he began to feel exhausted after Carnarvon's death and that exhaustion increased with the years. He finally went into a coma and died in the same Cairo hotel as had Carnarvon.

THE BETHELL CASE

Perhaps the strangest series of events connected with the curse began in 1929. Richard Bethell, the well-to-do son of a British lord, had been private secretary to Carnarvon and one of the first to enter the tomb. He was found dead in his bed one morning from a heart attack at the relatively young age of 46. Shortly after hearing the news, Bethell's father, Lord Westbury, committed suicide by leaping from the seventh story of his London townhouse. He left a note reading, "I really cannot stand any more horror and hardly see what good I am going to do here, so I am making my exit."[35]

Journalists jumped on the story. The United News Service reported that

> **DID YOU KNOW?**
> A British diplomat in Egypt in the 1920s wrote in his memoirs that Howard Carter, despite publicly scoffing at the idea of a curse, worried privately that Carnarvon's fate would be extended to him as a result of opening the tomb.

the seventy-eight-year old . . . had been worried about the death of his son, which occurred suddenly last November. Rumor attributed the young Bethell's death to the superstition which declares that those who violate the tomb will come to a violent end. Lord Westbury was frequently heard to mutter, "The curse of the pharaohs" as though this had preyed on his mind.[36]

As if this did not provide reporters enough for a sensational story, a third death came hard on the heels of the first two. As a hearse was transporting the body of Lord Westbury, it struck and killed eight-year-old Joseph Greer. Even what seemed a simple accident was attributed to the revenge of Tutankhamun.

Two More Deaths

The year 1934 saw two more deaths. The first was that of Arthur Weigall, who had a long history with Carter and the tomb. After studying Egyptology in Germany, Weigall went to work in England and then in Egypt for Flinders Petrie. He knew Carter well and, in fact, was Carter's replacement after the latter's dismissal in 1905 after the incident with French tourists.

Weigall's life took a far different turn during World War I, when he became a successful London stage designer and then a film critic for the London *Daily Mail*. In 1922 his combination of newspaper and Egyptology experience made him a natural to cover the Tutankhamun tomb story. He was outside the tomb on the day that the burial chamber was entered. To Weigall's thinking, it should have been a solemn occasion, but he noticed that Lord Carnarvon was laughing and joking. Weigall remarked to a fellow reporter, "If he goes down in that spirit, I give him six weeks to live."[37]

It was a far different Carnarvon who emerged from the tomb later that day. Weigall wrote, "Lord Carnarvon, always a delicate man, looked pale and exhausted as he came up out of the depths; and on the face of all those who had been present there were marks of fatigue and over-excitement."[38]

Weigall's death from undisclosed causes in January 1934 revived accounts of the curse, and those accounts quickly multiplied the next month when Albert Lythgoe, former head of the Egyptology exhibit at New York's Metropolitan Museum of Art, was hospitalized. When Lythgoe's wife ordered the hospital not to disclose the nature of his illness, the press linked it to the curse.

Winlock Takes a Stand

This was too much for Herbert Winlock, a successor of Lythgoe at the Metropolitan. He had refrained from speaking out about the curse, which he believed to be nonsense, but now thought the time had

THE CURSE GETS STRONG SUPPORT

Ｏne of the most ardent supporters of the idea that Tutankhamun's tomb was cursed was French Egyptologist J.S. Mardus. He based his belief on the fact that the tomb was the first largely intact royal tomb opened in modern times.

At a press conference in Paris in 1924, Mardus said that the tomb "contained, inviolate [undisturbed], all the things which the priests and masters of the funeral ceremony were able to place in the way of protection against profaners."

After the deaths of several people connected with the tomb, Mardus was asked his opinion:

> I am, unfortunately, not at all surprised. This is no childish superstition which can be dismissed with the shrug of a shoulder. We must remember that the Egyptians ... practiced magical rites the power of which held no doubts for them. I am absolutely convinced that they knew how to concentrate upon and around a mummy certain dynamic powers of which we possess very little in complete notions.

Quoted in Arnold C. Brackman, *The Search for the Gold of Tutankhamun*. New York: Mason/Charter, 1976, p. 163.

come. He held a press conference at which he pointed out that of the 40 people present at the opening of the inner tomb and sarcophagus, only 6 had died, and their average age had been 58. Also, he said, none of the 10 men present at the mummy's unwrapping had yet to die.

Winlock's views were duly reported, but they were quickly forgotten four days later when Lythgoe died and the curse story gained new life. Winlock's words would come back to haunt him, however, within a few years. Of the 10 living men he held up as disproving the curse, three were dead within four years: Callender in 1936 and both Carter and project photographer Harry Burton in 1939. Their deaths became part of the story of the curse even though all died of natural causes.

Worldwide interest in Tutankhamun and the curse waned with the onset of World War II but reemerged in the 1960s, when plans were being made for a large number of tomb artifacts to be exhibited out of the country. Mohammed Ibrahim, Egypt's director of antiquities, opposed sending the priceless objects abroad. He had had nightmares, he told government officials, about what would happen if the objects left the country. He was overruled nonetheless. Shortly afterward, Ibrahim stepped off a curb and was struck and killed by an automobile. According to some accounts, this accident occurred immediately after Ibrahim had left the meeting at which the final decision was made.

FATAL JOURNEY

Ibrahim's successor, Gamal Mehrez, had no qualms about shipping Tutankhamun's treasures to London for a later exhibition in 1972. Reminded by Vandenberg about the curse and Ibrahim's fate, Mehrez scoffed. "If you add up all these mysterious deaths, you might well think so," he said. "But I simply don't believe in it. Look at me. I've been involved with tombs and mummies of the pharaohs all my life. I'm living proof it was all coincidence."[39] Four weeks later Mehrez died suddenly at the age of 52. His death occurred on the same day that Tutankhamun's golden mask was packed for shipping.

Other mysterious occurrences surrounded that same shipment of artifacts. On the Royal Air Force plane carrying the treasures to England, one of the crew was said to have playfully kicked the crate carrying the golden mask and then joked that he had just kicked the world's most valuable object. As the story goes, he later broke the same leg he

Gamal Mehrez, Egypt's director of antiquities, died suddenly at the age of 52—on the same day that the golden funeral mask of Tutankhamun (pictured) was packed for shipment to an exhibition in London.

had used to kick the crate. Other members of the crew suffered heart attacks. The widow of one of the victims was quoted as saying that it had been Tutankhamun's curse that had killed her husband.

More recently, in 2009, a man named Carman Fields filed a lawsuit against Philadelphia's Franklin Institute Science Museum and Mandel

Center for injuries allegedly suffered while he was visiting an exhibition of objects from the tomb. According to his attorney, Fields "received a severe electrical shock and/or onslaught of dangerous, toxic and noxious chemicals emanating from the display that contacted him about the head and radiated into upper extremities, torso and lower extremities."[40] Fields sought $50,000 in damages, but the case was dismissed.

LADY ALMINA'S FATE

Perhaps the curse, if it exists, does not always involve death or physical injury. There have been other misfortunes as well. Following his death, Lord Carnarvon's widow, Lady Almina, quickly remarried. Her choice was the recently divorced Lieutenant Colonel Ian Dennistoun, who was then sued by his ex-wife who claimed he owed her a large sum of money. Lady Almina was called as a witness and was forced to confess that she had sold off jewelry and artwork to help support Dennistoun and to try to buy off the ex-wife.

The scandal and the loss of priceless family treasures caused Carnarvon's family to shun her. Her son, the new Lord Carnarvon, was so angry that he called her a "scheming swindler"[41] and ordered her favorite room at Highclere permanently locked. She was declared bankrupt at the age of 75 and wound up living in a small apartment that lacked hot water. She died in 1969 at the age of 93, choking on a bite of stew.

The argument over King Tut's curse has been raging for decades. Some blame the curse for the series of deaths that started with Lord Carnarvon. Others think it is complete nonsense—the result of overheated imaginations and overenthusiastic journalists. Still others acknowledge the deaths but try to find scientific explanations.

Many do not know what to think but do not see any reason to tempt fate. Carnarvon's son was interviewed by NBC Television in 1977 and was asked if he believed in the curse. He replied that he "neither believed it or disbelieved it," but he added that he "would not accept a million pounds to enter the tomb of Tutankhamun in the Valley of the Kings."[42]

CHAPTER 4

Natural or Supernatural?

Scholars and scientists have for decades routinely dismissed the idea of King Tut's curse as superstitious nonsense. They have yet, however, to come up with anything else that explains adequately all the deaths connected with the discovery. Was it mold, poisonous plants or animals, radioactivity, parasites, or gases? Was it simply a matter of coincidence? Or was it, after all, the magical power protecting the dead pharaoh reaching from the grave?

Magic played a major role in the everyday life of the ancient Egyptians, including in death. The word they used for magic was *heka*, and it was the underlying force that controlled both the world of the living and the underworld where the spirits of the dead were believed to reside.

Tutankhamun's journey into that underworld was liberally provided for, not only by food and drink left in the tomb but also by a host of god figures set there to keep watch and by more than 100 fetishes and amulets. Some of the gods were familiar to Howard Carter, but others were not. He wrote, "These comparatively inartistic figures of strange gods are valuable to us as a record of myths and beliefs, ritual and custom, associated with the dead. That they were supposed to be potent for good or evil, or have some form of magic inherent in them, is evident, although their exact meaning in this burial is not clear to us."[43]

MAGICAL OBJECTS

The tomb contained numerous fetishes—small carvings of animals or supernatural figures that were supposed to have special powers—and other objects that Egyptologist Nicholas Reeves has labeled "magical objects." The meanings of some of these items were clear. There were oars, for instance, to help Tutankhamun row himself through the underworld. Others were a mystery. As Reeves explains, "Their form is frequently as obscure as their significance."[44]

Survival of the body was a key element in the Egyptian view of death and was, indeed, the whole purpose of mummification. Additional protection was furnished—for the wealthy, at least—by amulets, or charms. Carter and his team found more than 140 of these small objects within the linen wrappings that encased the mummy. They were much more elaborate than the fetishes, and some were crafted from precious gems and metals. Carter wrote that there had very likely been many more within the nested coffins, but they had been taken away by tomb robbers.

Amulets were supposed to protect the various parts of the body next to which they had been placed. They took various shapes and colors, depending on what spirit was being invoked or how they were supposed to function. In their book on Egyptian funeral practices, Salima Ikram and Aidan Dodson write, "The power inherent in an amulet was transmitted not only by its shape, but also by its material and colour, all of which helped to endow the wearer with power, protection, and special capabilities."[45]

SPELLS OF POWER

Placing all of these figures, fetishes, and amulets in the tomb and within a mummy's wrappings was only part of the procedure. In or-

A guilded wooden statue of a hawk was among the many small carvings of animals and other figures found in the tomb of Tutankhamun. Objects such as these were thought by the ancient Egyptians to have special powers.

der for the object's *heka* to work its power, a spell was necessary. Such spells might be carved or written but were considered most powerful when spoken.

The large number of magical objects in Tutankhamun's tomb would have been thought to wield enormous power. This was usually the case when pharaohs died because they were considered gods, both on earth

THE RADIOACTIVITY THEORY

In 1949 Italian physicist Luis Bulgarini suggested that radioactivity may have contributed to Carnarvon's death and to the illnesses of others who spent time in Tutankhamun's tomb. "I believe that the ancient Egyptians understood the laws of atomic decay," he said. "Their priests and wise men were familiar with uranium. It is definitely possible that they used radiation in order to protect their holy places."

Bulgarini's idea was based on the fact that some matter occurring in nature, such as uranium, gives off radioactivity; in some cases, this process can last more than a billion years. "The floors of the tombs could have been covered with uranium or the graves could have been finished with radioactive rock," Bulgarini contended. "Such radiation could kill a man today or at least damage his health."

Exposure to radiation could account for at least one aspect of the mystery surrounding Tutankhamun's tomb. In the weeks before his death, Lord Carnarvon was reported to have lost some teeth. Tooth loss is, indeed, one symptom of radiation sickness, and it can be a sign of mercury poisoning as well. Subsequent tests, however, have found no trace of radiation in the tomb.

Philipp Vandenberg, *The Curse of the Pharaohs*. Philadelphia: J.B. Lippincott, 1975, p. 190.

and in the underworld. So, if there had been a curse such as the ones supposedly invoking death's wings, it would have been extremely potent.

The problem with this particular curse is that there is no reliable evidence that it ever existed. Moreover, it is not the kind of curse usually found on tombs. It threatens those who disturb the pharaoh's rest in very general terms, whereas most of the curses that have been found in tombs have been very specific as to what will befall the interloper. If anyone were to enter the tomb of the overseer Petety, for instance, "the priest of Hathor will beat twice any one of you who enters this tomb or does harm to it. The gods will confront him because I am honored by his Lord. The gods will not allow anything to happen to me. Anyone who does anything bad to my tomb, then the crocodile, the hippopotamus, and the lion will eat him."[46]

It was easy, however, for those who believed in the supernatural to think that Tutankhamun's tomb might have been cursed. After all, his tomb had been packed with magical objects and had survived relatively intact when so many others had been plundered. These facts, combined with the deaths of Carnarvon and others, made the curse story plausible for many.

THE SCIENTIFIC VIEW

In the interval between the time of Tutankhamun's death and AD 1922, however, science had largely supplanted superstition, and people began to look for other reasons for the rash of deaths. The first person to suggest that something other than a curse was at work was possibly Sir Arthur Conan Doyle. Although he had told a reporter that a curse was a possibility, he also said that Carnarvon's death might have been due to spores, which he called "elementals,"[47] having been placed in the tomb to infect the unwary robber.

The first person claiming to have found scientific proof that the tomb was, indeed, so infected was Ezzeddin Taha, a Cairo University biologist. Taha had conducted an extended study of respiratory illness among museum employees who worked with mummies and ancient artifacts. At a 1962 news conference he announced that he had confirmed the presence of *Aspergillus niger*, a fungus that can cause black mold, on the objects. Black mold spores, if inhaled, can sometimes cause fatal lung disease.

Taha did not claim that the spores had been placed in the tomb on purpose, only that they were present. Still, he said, "This discovery has once and for all destroyed the superstition that explorers who worked in ancient tombs died as a result of some kind of curse. . . . That belongs to the realm of fairy tales."[48]

Taha had little opportunity, however, to follow up on his discovery. Shortly after his news conference, the scientist and two assistants were killed in a head-on automobile collision. As Philipp Vandenberg put it, Taha had "become a victim of the curse he thought he had demystified."[49]

DEADLY MOLDS

The tomb toxin theory was revived in 1986, when French researcher Caroline Stenger-Phillip proposed that potentially deadly molds could have grown on the various foods placed in the tombs as offerings. Jennifer Wegner of the University of Pennsylvania Museum agreed. "When you think of Egyptian tombs, you have not only dead bodies but foodstuffs—meats, vegetables, and fruits," she said. "It certainly may have attracted insects, molds, [bacteria], and those kinds of things. The raw material would have been there thousands of years ago."[50]

Because the tombs were tightly sealed, Stenger-Phillip reasoned that mold spores could have remained active in dust particles. Then, when the tomb was entered centuries later and that dust was disturbed, toxic spores could have been inhaled.

In 1993 another toxic mold, *Aspergillus ochraceus*, was discovered at Egyptian archaeological sites by Italian physician Nicola Di Paolo. Di Paolo suggested that spores from the mold existed not only on tomb walls but also on objects in the tomb. Thus, it might be possible for the spores to infect people who had handled such objects even if they had not actually been in the tomb.

KRAMER'S STUDY

The next study was done by German microbiologist Gotthard Kramer in 1999. He examined 40 mummies and found, in addition to fungi previously reported, another strain far more dangerous: *Aspergillus flavus*. This mold produces a toxin known as aflatoxin, which is known to cause liver cancer. "When spores enter the body through the nose, mouth or eye mucous membranes," Kramer said, "they can lead to organ failure or even death, particularly in individuals with weakened immune systems."[51]

The various theories connecting King Tut's curse with fungi remain just that—theories. No direct link to any of the deaths has been proven. Furthermore, the fungi that were definitely found when Tutankhamun's tomb was opened were declared to be safe.

On the day after the tomb was opened in 1922, Alfred Lucas, a chemist on Carter's team, used cotton swabs to take samples from the walls and one of the shrines. "Fungus growths occur on the walls of the Burial Chamber, where they are so plentiful as to cause great disfigurement, and they occur also, though only to a slight extent, on the walls of the Antechamber and on the outside of the sarcophagus," Lucas wrote, "but in every instance the fungus is dry and apparently dead."[52] He was correct. The swabs were sent to a laboratory for an analysis that showed the fungi to be inactive.

> **DID YOU KNOW?**
> The so-called curse of King Tut received so much publicity in the 1920s that members of the US Congress suggested that hearings be held on any possible danger from mummies in American museums.

BACTERIAL INFECTION

If fungi were not the culprits of the curse, what about bacteria? Carter ruled them out, writing that "it may be accepted that no bacterial life whatsoever was present. The danger, therefore, to those working in the tomb from disease germs, against which they have been so frequently warned, is non-existent."[53]

Carter's opinion was based on the swabs, but it might have been difficult to generalize the absence of bacteria in an entire tomb from five swabs. In 1998 French scientist Sylvain Gandon suggested that spores different from those generated by fungi could have been the cause of Carnarvon's death. The death, he said, "could potentially be explained by infection with a highly virulent and very long-lived pathogen."[54]

A Canadian doctor, James McSherry, agreed and specifically mentioned anthrax as a possibility. "A malignant pustule in the oropharyngeal area [near the back of the throat] would well produce an illness similar to the tragic event that caused Lord Carnarvon's demise," he said, adding that

> anthrax certainly existed in ancient times and is often assumed to have been responsible for the fifth and sixth plagues of Egypt [that caused livestock disease and incurable skin boils], which are well described in chapter nine of Exodus [in the Bible]. Anthrax spores could have well been present in the tomb, and there would have been a real risk of exposure once the ancient dust was stirred.[55]

Yet if Carnarvon died of anthrax, why did the disease, which is almost always fatal, strike no one else?

ANIMAL WASTE

Animal waste has also been put forward as a candidate for whatever struck Carnarvon and some of the others. In his book, Vandenberg cites the case of a geologist who, while exploring a cave in what is now the African country of Zimbabwe, was suddenly surrounded by a horde of bats. He fell ill shortly thereafter, complaining of aching, fever, and indigestion—symptoms that had been reported by some archaeologists in Egypt.

The geologist's disease was diagnosed as histoplasmosis, a potentially fatal disease transmitted by a fungus in bat droppings. One of his doctors, Geoffrey Dean, suggested that the same disease might have killed Carnarvon and sickened others. He discovered from a colleague in Egypt that bats had indeed been a problem in Tutankhamun's tomb in the 1920s. They flew in at night through a temporary door made of iron bars during the six months before a more permanent door was installed. According to Dean,

> We may never know for certain, but the evidence suggests that Lord Carnarvon's death was due to inhalation of dust contain-

DEADLY WRAPPINGS?

Although most speculation on the curse of King Tut has centered on possibly harmful substances left in the tomb, it has also been suggested that poisons might have been in and around the mummy itself. In describing the various ingredients used in the mummification process, Philipp Vandenberg writes, "Today we know a great deal about the botanical and pharmaceutical composition of the ingredients used in mummification, but we don't know everything."

What is known, however, is that the Egyptians knew how to distill the seeds of various fruits to produce hydrogen cyanide, also known as prussic acid, the same substance that was used in the Nazi death camps during World War II. Some experts believe that a weakened form of this deadly poison was used to coat the linen wrappings of mummies in order to better preserve them.

Philipp Vandenberg, *The Curse of the Pharaohs*. Philadelphia: J.B. Lippincott, 1975, p. 133.

ing the fungus *histoplasma* from the dried bat droppings in the passage leading to King Tutankhamun's tomb. His death so soon after opening the burial chapter and the reported unexpected deaths of Arthur Mace and Georges Benedite . . . led to the persisting belief in the legend of the Curse of the Pharaohs.[56]

DELIBERATE ACTIONS

Although many of the tomb toxin theories suggest ways in which deaths might have occurred due to natural causes, others take up another question: Were the deaths caused by some substance deliberately placed in the tomb by ancient Egyptian priests? As Vandenberg writes, "If we assume that the curse of the pharaohs was specifically designed to protect the royal tomb, these matters would not have been left to chance. Poison is a much more realistic theory."[57]

The ancient Egyptians certainly had no lack of poisons from which to choose. There were then, as now, scorpions everywhere. The cobra was a source of poison, as was the asp—the small but highly venomous snake with which Cleopatra was supposed to have killed herself. Also, more than 300 species of spiders live in Egypt, and several of them are poisonous, such as the white widow. Toads in the Nile Delta secrete a number of toxic substances from glands on humps behind their ears.

Among the many beetles to be found in Egypt is *Lytta vesicatoria*, commonly known as the Spanish fly. When dried and crushed, it produces a powder that can cause inflammation on the skin. If the powder is taken internally, it can cause severe kidney damage. These effects were described by the Greek physician Hippocrates as far back as 400 BC and likely were known to the Egyptians as well.

POTENT POISONS

Also perhaps present in Tutankhamun's time, although not native to Egypt, was *Diamphidia simplex*, a leaf beetle native to southern Africa. Bushmen of the Kalahari Desert would squeeze the larvae of this beetle, thereby producing a highly lethal poison that they could use on their arrows. In some cases the potency of this poison is increased by mixing it with juices from the plant *Haemanthus toxicarius*, otherwise known as the bloodflower. Although *Diamphidia simplex* and *Haemanthus toxicarius* are not native to Egypt, it is possible that their poisons were imported as part of the thriving trade with lands to the south.

In 1962 an Egyptian biologist announced that he had disproved the curse when he confirmed the potentially deadly presence of the fungus Aspergillus niger *(pictured in a colored scanning electron micrograph) on objects from Tut's tomb. Shortly after his announcement, he died in a car crash.*

Such poisons, if placed in ancient tombs, might well have retained their potency over the centuries. Louis Lewin, a German scientist who studied poisons, reported analyzing traces found on arrows almost 100 years old. "The poison in the arrows is as potent as if it had been freshly made,"[58] he wrote.

Another poisonous plant from southern Africa, the jequirity bean, could have followed the same trade route. These bright red beans, often used for necklaces, contain the toxin abrin, a tiny quantity of which can cause red blood cells to break down and clot. Closer to Egypt, near the upper reaches of the Nile River, the vine *Strophanthus* produces a poison that works by disrupting heart function. Famous explorer David Livingstone reported that arrows bearing this poison are able to cause death in animals as large as the elephant.

NATIVE POISONS

This is not to say that there are no poisonous plants native to Egypt. The first known pharaoh, Menes, is supposed to have grown poisonous plants, but exactly what they were is unknown. Ancient texts, however, describe poisons whose effects are the same as those of hemlock, henbane, and monkshood—all of which can be fatal if ingested.

Some poisons, however, do not need to be swallowed and can enter the body through a cut or piercing. The poison in jequirity beans, for example, can be absorbed by perspiration if handled. Other lethal substances likewise can cause harm through contact, and some of these were likely present in the tomb. The Egyptians included such powerful poisons as aconite, arsenic, and hemlock in the paints used to adorn artifacts and walls.

> ### DID YOU KNOW?
> A study by professional magician and author James Randi showed that the 23 people most intimately involved with Tutankhamun's tomb lived, on average, 24 additional years after exposure to the tomb and died at an average age of 73.

It has also been suggested that one way to safeguard a tomb was the use of candles whose wicks were soaked in arsenic. The candles would be lit just before the final closing of the tomb; as they burned, poisonous vapors would be given off. Such vapors would settle on objects and, in an airtight setting, would remain until handled.

Although no candle remnants were found in Tutankhamun's tomb, there were poisons there that could be transmitted by touch. There were many weapons, including bows, arrows, knives, and swords, and like the majority of cutting weapons of the time, most were made of bronze. Bronze is an alloy that is 85 to 95 percent copper mixed with another metal, usually tin. Egyptian armorers, however, used arsenic for the other 15 to 5 percent. Arsenic also was used to make the paint that decorated the walls of the tomb.

A LACK OF PROOF

Despite all the conjecture, there is no proof that anything in Tutankhamun's tomb—fungi, poisons, or bacteria—played any role in the death of Lord Carnarvon. F. DeWolfe Miller, a professor of epidemiology at the University of Hawaii, said that his opinion matched that of Howard Carter. Carter once remarked that, given the unsanitary conditions of Egypt in the 1920s, it was probably safer inside the tomb than outside. "The idea that an underground tomb, after 3,000 years, would have some kind of bizarre microorganism in it that's going to kill somebody six weeks later . . . is very hard to believe."[59]

Vandenberg argues otherwise. He contends that science has shown that mold spores and bacteria can last almost indefinitely, and as for poisons,

> the shriveling of poisonous glands or the drying up of poisons themselves does not decrease their potency. Not even a marked change in temperature weakens cobra poison; after a fifteen minute exposure to 100-degree-centigrade temperatures, the venom retains full potency. Snake poisons with a protein base, on the other hand, are not as resistant; they lose their effectiveness at 75 to 80 degrees centigrade, as do certain insect poisons. Ultraviolet rays can also neutralize insect poisons, but the pharaohs' tombs, which these rays cannot penetrate, would have made ideal places for storing such poisons and keeping their effectiveness unimpaired.[60]

A MATTER OF COINCIDENCE

The best explanation for the curse of King Tut's tomb, however, may be that there never was such a thing—that all the supposedly mysterious deaths have been a matter of coincidence and have not been all that out of the ordinary. In 2002 Mark R. Nelson of Monash University in Australia undertook the same type of study as had Herbert Winlock in 1934.

He compiled a list of 44 people from the United States and Europe who were in Egypt at the time of the tomb's discovery. Twenty-five had had direct exposure to the tomb or the mummy and might be considered logical targets of a curse. The other 19 were not exposed.

No significant difference was found in the life spans of the individuals in the two groups. Their average age at time of death was 70.

A statistical analysis of his findings showed a 95 percent chance that a difference in the survival rates of the exposed and unexposed groups was coincidental and would have occurred anyway. "The Egyptian archaeological dig in the 1920s was inhabited by interesting characters and it was this, and the circumstances of the most important archaeological find of the modern age, that has kept the myth of the mummy's curse in the public eye," Nelson explains. "I found no evidence for its existence. Perhaps finally it, like the tragic boy king Tutankhamun, may be put to rest."[61]

A FICKLE CURSE

The curse had, indeed, been peculiarly selective in its victims. Why would the spirits that protected the dead Tutankhamun strike down an 8-year-old boy in England but spare Douglas Derry, the man who dissected his mummy and survived to the age of 87? What about Carnarvon's daughter, Lady Evelyn? She was one of the first three people to enter the tomb and lived to be 78. Most of all, what about Howard Carter, without whom the tomb might never have been discovered, and who died at age 66 at a time when the average life span for men was 62?

But, despite all arguments, scientific investigations, and mathematical analyses, the story of King Tut's curse lives on. Like the villain in a string of horror movies, it refuses to die. As recently as 2005, unexplained events surrounded the mummy. While Ashraf Salim was performing the first-ever computed tomography (CT) scan on Tutankhamun's mummy, he related that there had been "several strange occurrences. The electricity suddenly went out, the CT scanner could not be started and a team member became ill. If we weren't scientists, we might have become believers in the Curse of the Pharaohs."[62]

SOURCE NOTES

INTRODUCTION: DEATH AND HIS LORDSHIP

1. Quoted in James M. Deem, "Was the Curse of King Tut's Tomb Caused by Anthrax?," Mummy Tombs. http://mummytombs.com.
2. Quoted in Philipp Vandenberg, *The Curse of the Pharaohs*. Philadelphia: J.B. Lippincott, 1975, p. 24.
3. Quoted in Vandenberg, *The Curse of the Pharaohs*, p. 25.

CHAPTER ONE: THE BOY KING

4. Quoted in Christine El Mahdy, *Tutankhamun: The Life and Death of the Boy King*. New York: St. Martin's, pp. 86–89.
5. Quoted in Ker Than, "King Tut Mysteries Solved: Was Disabled, Malarial, and Inbred," *National Geographic News*, February 16, 2010. http://news.nationalgeographic.com.
6. Zahi Hawass, "King Tut's Family Secrets," *National Geographic*, September 2010. http://ngm.nationalgeographic.com.

CHAPTER TWO: SEARCH AND DISCOVERY

7. Quoted in Arnold C. Brackman, *The Search for the Gold of Tutankhamun*. New York: Mason/Charter, 1976, p. 26.
8. Quoted in Nicholas Reeves, *The Complete Tutankhamun*. London: Thames and Hudson, 1990, p. 38.
9. Quoted in Thomas Hoving, *Tutankhamun: The Untold Story*. New York: Simon and Schuster, 1978, p. 25.
10. Quoted in Brackman, *The Search for the Gold of Tutankhamun*, p. 64.
11. Quoted in Howard Carter and A.C. Mace, *The Discovery of the Tomb of Tutankhamen*. New York: Dover, 1977, p. 87.
12. Quoted in Hoving, *Tutankhamun*, p. 76.
13. Howard Carter, *The Tomb of Tutankhamen*. New York: Excalibur, 1972, p. 32.
14. Quoted in Hoving, *Tutankhamun*, p. 81.

15. Quoted in Hoving, *Tutankhamun*, p. 82.
16. Quoted in Andrew Collins and Chris Ogilvie-Herald, *Tutankhamun: The Exodus Conspiracy*. London: Virgin, 2002, p. 41.
17. Quoted in Carter, *The Tomb of Tutankhamun*, p. 35.
18. Quoted in Hoving, *Tutankhamun*, p. 88.
19. Carter and Mace, *The Discovery of the Tomb of Tutankhamen*, p. 101.
20. Quoted in Brackman, *The Search for the Gold of Tutankhamun*, p. 109.

CHAPTER THREE: THE STORY TAKES HOLD

21. Quoted in Lisa Hopkins, "Jane C. Loudon's 'The Mummy!' Mary Shelley Meets George Orwell and They Go in a Balloon to Egypt," *Cardiff Corvey: Reading the Romantic Text*, no. 10, June 2003, Cardiff University. www.cf.ac.uk.
22. Quoted in Deem, "Was the Curse of King Tut's Tomb Caused by Anthrax?"
23. Quoted in Henry Herbert, Earl of Carnarvon, *No Regrets: The Memoirs of the Earl of Carnarvon*. London: Weidenfeld and Nicolson, 1976, p. 125.
24. Quoted in Herbert, *No Regrets*, p. 127.
25. Quoted in Collins and Ogilvie-Herald, *Tutankhamun*, p. 85.
26. Quoted in Collins and Ogilvie-Herald, *Tutankhamun*, p. 80.
27. Quoted in Herbert, *No Regrets*, p. 122.
28. Quoted in Carter and Mace, *The Discovery of the Tomb of Tutankhamen*, p. 163.
29. Quoted in John Warren, "The Mummy's Curse," Tour Egypt. www.touregypt.net.
30. Vandenberg, *The Curse of the Pharaohs*, p. 20.
31. Quoted in John Lawton, "The Last Survivor," *Saudi Aramco World*, November/December 1981. www.saudiaramcoworld.com.
32. Quoted in Collins and Ogilvie-Herald, *Tutankhamun*, p. 89.
33. Quoted in Hoving, *Tutankhamun*, p. 227.
34. Quoted in "Victims of the Curse of King Tut." http://www.king-tut.org.uk/curse-of-king-tut/victims-of-the-curse-of-king-tut.htm.

35. Quoted in Lee Krystek, "Howard Carter and the 'Curse of the Mummy,'" *Museum of Unnatural Mystery*. http://unmuseum.org.

36. Quoted in Collins and Ogilvie-Herald, *Tutankhamun*, p. 122.

37. Quoted in Julie Hankey, *Arthur Weigall, Tutankhamun, and the "Curse of the Pharaohs."* London: Tauris Parke, 2007, p. 5.

38. Quoted in Collins and Ogilvie-Herald, *Tutankhamun*, p. 122.

39. Quoted in Vandenberg, *The Curse of the Pharaohs*, p. 11.

40. Quoted in Michael Klein, "Newest Eagle Eyes Bryn Mawr," *Philadelphia Inquirer*, August 16, 2010. www.allbusiness.com.

41. Quoted in Christopher Wilson, "Dark Past of the Real Downton Abbey Duchess," *Telegraph*, August 9, 2011. www.telegraph.co.uk.

42. Quoted in Hoving, *Tutankhamun*, p. 229.

CHAPTER FOUR: NATURAL OR SUPERNATURAL?

43. Quoted in Reeves, *The Complete Tutankhamun*, p. 133.

44. Reeves, *The Complete Tutankhamun*, p. 135.

45. Salima Ikram and Aidan Dodson, *The Mummy in Ancient Egypt*. London: Thames and Hudson, 1998, p. 137.

46. Quoted in Larry Orcutt, "Curses!," Catchpenny Mysteries of Ancient Egypt, 2000. www.catchpenny.org.

47. Quoted in Brackman, *The Search for the Gold of Tutankhamun*, p. 113.

48. Quoted in Vandenberg, *The Curse of the Pharaohs*, p. 169.

49. Quoted in Vandenberg, *The Curse of the Pharaohs*, p. 170.

50. Quoted in Brian Handwerk, "Egypt's 'King Tut Curse' Caused by Tomb Toxins?," *National Geographic News*, May 6, 2005. http://news.nationalgeographic.com.

51. Quoted in Krystek, "Howard Carter and the 'Curse of the Mummy.'"

52. Quoted in Andrew Collins, "The True Curse of the Mummy—Bram Stoker, Whitby, and the Death of Lord Carnarvon," Andrew Collins.com, January 5, 2003. www.andrewcollins.com.

53. Quoted in Collins, "The True Curse of the Mummy."

54. Quoted in Gil Kezwer, "King Tut's Curse Due to Fatal Spores?," *Canadian Medical Association Journal*, December 15, 1988. www.collectionscanada.gc.ca.

55. Quoted in Qualtest, "Is the 'King Tut Curse' Caused by Toxins Produced by Microorganisms?," www.qualtestusa.com/KingTutsCurse.html.

56. Geoffrey Dean, *The Turnstone: A Doctor's Story*. Liverpool, UK: Liverpool University Press, 2002, p. 96.

57. Vandenberg, *The Curse of the Pharaohs*, p. 172.

58. Quoted in Vandenberg, *The Curse of the Pharaohs*, p. 176.

59. Quoted in Brian Handwerk, "Curse of the Mummy," *National Geographic*. http://science.nationalgeographic.com.

60. Vandenberg, *The Curse of the Pharaohs*, p. 176.

61. Mark R. Nelson, "The Mummy's Curse: Historical Cohort Study," *British Medical Journal,* December 21, 2002. www.bmj.com.

62. Quoted in Rashmi Yadav, "Inside the Head of an Ancient Pharaoh," RxPG News, November 28, 2006. www.rxpgnews.com.

FOR FURTHER RESEARCH

BOOKS

Norman Bancroft-Hunt, *Living in Ancient Egypt*. New York: Chelsea House, 2009.

Mark Beynon, *London's Curse: Murder, Black Magic and Tutankhamun in the 1920s West End*. Charleston, SC: History Press, 2012.

Bob Brier and Hoyt Hobbs, *Daily Life of the Ancient Egyptians*. Westport, CT: Greenwood, 2008.

Zahi Hawass, *Tutankhamun: The Golden King and the Great Pharaohs*. Washington, DC: National Geographic, 2008.

T.G.H. James, *Howard Carter: The Path to Tutankhamun*. New York: Tauris Parke, 2012.

Daniel Meyerson, *In the Valley of the Kings: Howard Carter and the Mystery of King Tutankhamun's Tomb*. New York: Ballantine, 2009.

WEBSITES

Ancient Egypt: The Mythology (www.egyptianmyths.net). This site is devoted to the ancient Egyptian religion and features sections on gods, myths, and symbols. It also has links to Egyptian collections in major museums.

The Animal Mummy Project (www.animalmummies.com/project .html). This project undertaken by the Cairo Museum deals with why and how animals were mummified in ancient Egypt. Some animals were cherished pets; others had religious significance.

Development of Pyramids Gallery (www.bbc.co.uk/history/ancient /egyptians). This site, part of the British Broadcasting Corporation's

History series, traces ancient Egyptian tombs from prehistoric pit burials through the New Kingdom pyramids.

The Griffith Institute (www.griffith.ox.ac.uk/tutankhamundiscovery .html). This institute was established in 1939 as the University of Oxford's Egyptology center. Its "Tutankhamun: Anatomy of an Excavation" provides a detailed archaeological record of Howard Carter and Lord Carnarvon's discovery of the tomb of Tutankhamun.

KingTutOne (www.kingtutone.com). This site is devoted entirely to Tutankhamun and includes a spectacular tour through a virtual tomb.

Metropolitan Museum of Art (www.metmuseum.org/toah/hd/tuta /hd_tuta.htm). The Department of Egyptian Art discusses some puzzling features of Tutankhamun's funeral. The site also includes a slideshow of Tut artifacts.

National Geographic Magazine (http://ngm.nationalgeographic .com/2005/06/king-tut/mysteries/home). In its "Unraveling the Mysteries of King Tutankhamun," this site presents an interactive expedition into the discovery of King Tut's tomb and a link to the magazine's earlier story, "The New Face of King Tut."

Pyramids: The Inside Story (www.pbs.org/wgbh/nova/pyramid). This site is based on the episode of the Public Broadcasting System's *NOVA* series dealing with the Great Pyramids of Giza. It includes information on how the pyramids were constructed and interviews with archaeologists.

Theban Mapping Project (www.thebanmappingproject.com). Produced by the Theban Foundation, this site features interactive atlases of the Valley of the Kings and the entire complex of tombs in and around ancient Thebes.

Tutankhamun and the Golden Age of the Pharaohs (http://archive .fieldmuseum.org/tut/story.asp). In "The Story of King Tut," the Field Museum of Natural History in Chicago discusses all aspects of Tutankhumun's life and death as well as life in Egypt during the time of the pharaohs. The information found on this site accompanied the museum's King Tut exhibition.

INDEX

Note: Boldface page numbers indicate illustrations.

Adamson, Richard, 26, 46
aflatoxin, 60–61
afterlife 21, 33
Ahmose (pharaoh), 10
Akhenaten (Amenhotep IV, pharoah), 11,
   13–14, 15, 18
Akhetaten ("Horizon of the Aten"), 11,
   13, 18
Alcott, Louisa May, 41
Almina, Lady, 8–9, 54
Amenhotep III (pharaoh), 11, 13
Amenhotep IV (pharaoh), 11, 13
amulets, 55, 56
Amun (Amen, god)
   Amenhotep IV (Akhenaten) and, 11
   coronation of pharaohs and, 16
   Opet festival, 20–22
   Tutankhamun and, 13, 15–16
Amun-Ra (god), 11
animal waste, 62–63
Ankhesenpaaten (Ankhesenamun)
   marriage of, 18
   new name of, 22
   parents of, 16
anthrax, 62
arsenic, 66
Aspergillus flavus, 60–61
Aspergillus niger, 59, **65**
Aspergillus ochraceus, 60
Atef crown, 16
Aten (god), 11, 18–19
Ay
   Akhenaten and, 14
   Horemheb and, 15, 18, 24
   religion and, 15
   Tutankhamun and, 18, 22
Ayrton, Edward, 41

bacteria, 61–62, 67

Belzoni, Giovanni, 41
Benedite, Georges, 47, 63
Bethell, Richard, 9, 49
bird curses, 43
black land, 16
black mold, 59
Blue Crown, 16–17, **17**
Book of the Dead, **48**
Breasted, James, 36
Bulgarini, Luis, 58
Burton, Harry, 52

Callender, A.R. "Pecky"
   death of, 52
   discovery of tomb and, 33, 35
   viewing of tomb by, 38
Capart, Jean, 28, 45
Carnarvon, Evelyn (daughter)
   death of, 68
   viewing of tomb by, 36, 38–39
Carnarvon, Henry (son)
   death of father and, 9, 41–42, 43, 44
   mother and, 54
   opinion of curse, 54
Carnarvon, Lord
   background of, 25, 29–30
   Carter and
      exploration of tomb by, 36–39
      financing by, 32
      notification of tomb discovery, 35
      partnership of, 30

   death of, 8–9, 39, 41–43, 58
   Egyptian nickname for, 6
   health of, 6, 8
   occult and, 43
   warning given to, 44–45

Carter, Howard
   background of, 25–29
   Carnarvon and
      death of, 9, 39, 42–43

financing by, 32
partnership of, 30
characteristics of, 26
Davis and, 27
death of, 52, 68
good luck symbol of, 32
tomb of Thutmosis IV and, 29
Tutankhamun's tomb and
curse and, 41, 45–46, 49
on deadly substances in, 61, 67
digging strategy of , 31
discovery of, 6, 33–34, 35
exploration of, 36–39
on unknown gods, 55
Champollion, Jean-François, 41
Chiero, 43–44
cobras, 35–36
Corelli, Marie, 8, 45
crowns, 16–17, **17**
Curse of the Pharaohs, The (Vandenberg), 45
curses
associated with mummies, 40–41
found in tombs, 43, 45, 58–59
most common ancient Egyptian, 46
as spells, 57–58
curses on tomb of Tutankhamun
Carter and, 41, 45–46, 49
challenge for proof of, 45
Corelli and, 8, 45
deaths supposedly related to, 50, 52, 53
Carnarvon, 8–9, 39, 41–43, 58
Ember family, 46–47
Taha, 60
visitors, 46–47, 48–49
Winlock's statistics and, 50–52
newspapers and, 46, 48, 49, 50
as protection, 46

Davis, Theodore
artifacts found by, 30, 31–32
Carter and, 27
deaths of team members of, 41
end of digging by, 31
tomb of Horemheb and, 29
Valley of the Kings and, 27–29, 30–31
Dean, Geoffrey, 62–63
death/deaths

ancient Egyptian beliefs about, 55–56
expeditions to Egypt and, 41
longevity and tomb exposure, 51, 66, 68
scientific explanations for
animal waste, 62–63
bacteria, 61–62
molds, 59–61
radioactivity, 58
supposedly related to curse, 50, 52, 53
Carnarvon, 8–9, 39, 41–43, 58
Ember family, 46–47
Taha, 60
visitors, 46–47, 48–49
Winlock's statistics and, 50–52
Dennistoun, Ian, 54
Derry, Douglas, 68
Di Paolo, Nicola, 60
DNA, 13, 22–23
Dodson, Aidan, 56
Doyle, Sir Arthur Conan, 46, 59

Egypt, 10, **12**, 26
See also pharaohs
Egyptian Antiquities Service, 27, 29, 38
Eighteenth Dynasty, 10, 24
Elizabeth (queen of Belgium), 38
El Mahdy, Christine, 24
Ember, Aaron, 47–48
Evelyn-White, Hugh, 47
exhibitions, 52, 53–54

fetishes, 55–56
Fields, Carman, 53–54
fungi, 59–61, 63

Gandon, Sylvain, 61
Gardiner, Alan, 45
Golden Bird, 32, 35–36
Gould, George Jay, 46–47
Greer, Joseph, 50

Hamon, Count Louis le Warner, 43–44
Hawass, Zahi, 23
Heka (magic), 55
Herbert, Aubrey, 47
Herbert, George Edward Stanhope
Molyneux. *See* Carnarvon, Lord
hieroglyphics, 26

Hippocrates, 64
histoplasmosis, 62–63
Hittites, 18, 20
Horemheb
    Akhenaten and, 14
    armies of, 18–19
    as king, 24
    religion and, 15
    tomb of, 29
    Tutankhamun and, 18
hydrogen cyanide, 63

Ibrahim, Mohammed, 52
Ikram, Salima, 56
insects, 60, 64, 67

jequirity beans, 65, 66
Joel, Woolf, 47
Jones, Ernest Harold, 41

Karnak, 11, 15, 20–21
Kepresh (crown), 16–17, **17**
Khrushchev, Nikita, 64
Kiya, 13
Kramer, Gotthard, 60–61

Land of Punt, 56
leaf beetles, 64
Lewin, Louis, 65
Livingstone, David, 65
Lordy. *See* Carnarvon, Lord
Lower Egypt, **12**, 16
Lucas, Alfred, 61
Lythgoe, Albert, 50, 52

Mace, Arthur C., 48–49, 63
Mackay, Mary. *See* Corelli, Marie
magic
    importance of, 55
    Khrushchev and, 64
    objects associated with, 56–58, **57**
    spells, 57–58
malaria, 23
Mardus, J.S., 51
Maspero, Sir Gaston, 27, 29
McSherry, James, 62
Mehrez, Gamal, 52
Merton, Arthur, 34

Miller, F. DeWolfe, 67
molds, 59–61, **65**, 67
mummification
    ingredients used in, 56, 63
    process described, 21
    purpose of, 56
    of Tutankhamun, 19, 23, 68
    US Congress and, 61
Mummy, The (children's book), 40

Nefertiti, 13, 15
Nelson, Mark R., 67–68
Newberry, Percy, 25–26
newspapers
    curses and, 45–46, 48, 49, 50
    London Times, 28
    telegraph and, 30
New York Times (newspaper), 8
Nineteenth Dynasty, 24

occult, 43
Opet festival, 20–21
Osiris (god), **17**

Petrie, Flinders, 26, 29, 48
pharaohs
    after Tutankhamun, 24
    before Tutankhamun, 10–11, 13–14
    cobras as symbol of, 35–36
    coronation names, 14
    preservation and burial of, 21
    See also tombs; Valley of the Kings;
        specific kings
plants, poisonous, 65–66
poisons, 63, 64–66, 67
Pusch, Carsten, 22–23

radioactivity, 58Ramesses X, 13
Randi, James, 66
Red Crown, 16
red land, 16
Reed, Archibald Douglas, 47
Reeves, Nicholas, 56
religion
    after Akhenaten, 15–16
    Akhenaten and, 11, 13–14
    Opet festival, 20–22
    Tutankhamun and, 18–19

unknown gods, 55
Restoration Stele, 15, 18
Rosetta stone, 26, 41, **42**

Salim, Ashraf, 68
shabbats, 33
Smenkhkare, 14–15
snakes, 64, 67
Spanish flies, 64
spores, 59–61
Stenger-Phillip, Caroline, 60
Stoker, Bram, 41
Strophanthus, 65

Taha, Ezzeddin, 59–60
Thutmose I, 10, 11, 13
Thutmose IV (pharaoh), 29
Times (London), 28, 34
toads, 64
tombs
    discoveries of, 29, 41
    location of, 16
    plunder of, 24, 28, 29, 35
    See also Tutankhamun's tomb; Valley of
        the Kings
toxins, 59–61, 63–65
Tutankhamun (King Tut), **17**
    birth of, 13
    coronation of, 14, 16–18
    death of, 22–23
    funeral mask of, 53
    health of, 10
    mummification of
        CT scan of, 68
        daughters of, 23
        head, 19 (illustration)
        names of, 14, 21–22
        parents of, 11, 13
        religion and, 15–16, 18–19
Tutankhamun's tomb, **7, 37**
    deaths supposedly related to, 50, 52, 53
        Carnarvon, 8–9, 39, 41–43, 58
        Ember family, 46–47

Taha, 60
    visitors, 46–47, 48–49
    Winlock's statistics and, 50–52
    discovery of, 6, 33–34
    guards, 26
    injuries supposedly related to, 52–54
    location of, 24
    size and condition of, 23–24

underworld, 55, 56
Upper Egypt, **12**, 16
    See also Valley of the Kings
US Congress, 61

Valley of the Kings, **27**
    Davis and, 27–29, 30–31
    digging strategy of Carter and
        Carnarvon, 31
    first and last pharaohs buried in, 13

Vandenberg, Philipp
    on Carnarvon's death, 62
    on curse in tomb, 45
    on death of Taha, 60
    on ingredients used in mummification,
        63
    on poison in tomb, 64, 67

War Crown, 16–17, **17**
Warner, William, 43–44
Wegner, Jennifer, 60
Weigall, Arthur, 50
Westbury, Lord, 49–50
White Crown, 16, 17
Winlock, Herbert
    on death of Golden Bird, 35–36
    expedition to Tutankhamun's tomb and,
        48
    location of Tutankhamun's tomb and,
        31–32
    statistics about curse, 50–52

Younger Lady (mother of Tut), 13

PICTURE CREDITS

ABOUT THE AUTHOR

William W. Lace is a native of Fort Worth, Texas. He retired in 2011 after 30 years as an administrator at Tarrant County College and now teaches journalism there. He holds a bachelor's degree from Texas Christian University, a master's degree from East Texas State University, and a doctorate from the University of North Texas. Prior to joining Tarrant County College, he was director of the news service at the University of Texas at Arlington and a sportswriter and columnist for the *Fort Worth Star-Telegram*. He has written more than 50 nonfiction books for young readers on subjects ranging from the atomic bomb to the Dallas Cowboys. He and his wife, Laura, a retired school librarian, live in Arlington, Texas, and have two children and four grandchildren.